AROUND IRELAND ON A BIKE

Paul Benjaminse

THE O'BRIEN PRESS
DUBLIN

Acknowledgements

I would first of all like to thank Kathryn Callaghan, who persuaded me to discover Northern Ireland – she and her colleague Beverley Pierson really opened my eyes to Ulster. Yvonne Zuidema of Ireland Tourism helped me immensely with the route in the Republic of Ireland; without her enthusiasm and perseverance it would not have been possible to plan the route as smoothly as we did. Needless to say, this also applies to her colleagues in Ireland. Annet, Arnoud and Barry were once again wonderfully helpful to me in producing the maps. Arnold set a new standard for displaying relief on maps, while Barry was inspired by Celtic motifs in designing the layout of the publication and Annet, as always, was a meticulous editor and proof-reader. I look forward to meeting up with all of you soon to enjoy a 'pint of the black stuff'. Finally, I would like to thank Karin for putting up with my moods as I worked away at my Mac all those evenings and weekends. I hope we will have the opportunity to visit Ireland many more times in the future.

Kindest regards

Paul Benjaminse
cycling@cyclingeurope.nl
www.cyclingeurope.nl

This edition first published 2012
by The O'Brien Press Ltd,
12 Terenure Road East,
Rathgar,
Dublin 6,
Ireland.
Tel: +353 1 4923333;
Fax: +353 1 4922777
E-mail: books@obrien.ie
Website: www.obrien.ie

ISBN: 978-1-84717-309-6

Text and illustrations © copyright Benjaminse Uitgeverij 2012
Front cover photograph courtesy of iStockphoto.
First published in the Dutch language by Benjaminse Uitgeverij in 2009
Copyright for typesetting, layout, editing, design © The O'Brien Press Ltd

Thanks to Fáilte Ireland for supporting the translation of this work.

All rights reserved.
No part of this publication may be reproduced or utilised in any form or by any means, electronic or mechanical, including photocopying, recording or in any information storage and retrieval system, without permission in writing from the publisher.
British Library Cataloguing-in-Publication Data
A catalogue record for this title is available from The British Library

1 2 3 4 5 6 7 8
12 13 14 15 16

Printed and bound by KHL Printing, Singapore.
The paper used in this book is produced using pulp from managed forests.

TABLE OF CONTENTS

4	Why would someone embark on a bicycle tour of Ireland?
5	Season, climate, accommodation, food and preparation
7	Transport
7	The entire tour, half, or the other way around?
9	Chapter 1 *Ulster*
34	Chapter 2 *Sligo*
36	Chapter 3 *A taste of Connemara*
60	Chapter 4 *To The Burren*
68	Chapter 5 *Kerry and Dingle*
85	Chapter 6 *Cork and the South East*
118	Chapter 7 *Mount Leinster, Wicklow and Dublin*
123	Final note

Why would someone embark on a bicycle tour of Ireland?

Because Ireland is as stunning a country as any you'll ever visit. There's the extraordinary light, which adds intensity to everything, making greens and whites appear greener and whiter. It's all there: dark green mountains rising ominously from the mist, bright blue skies over white sandy beaches; the ghostlike ruins of ancient monasteries on misty days ...

Ireland is steeped in history: the Celts and the monks, the years of domination, oppression, uprising and rebellion; martyrs and refugees. Ireland is also traditionally a country marked by faith and strength of will, sometimes against the people's own better judgment. Resilience is ingrained in the Irish character: it has taught them a profound sense of self-respect during times of poverty, and it is that self-respect that strikes you as a visitor when interacting with the people. Take time to listen to people's stories and the music they play in even the smallest pubs. There's tremendous strength in this country, strength the people need time and again to fight back.

Is Ireland a cycling country?

Absolutely. Although there are only a handful of areas that attract large numbers of cyclists, it is an ideal biking destination once you've worked out what roads to take. The regular thoroughfares are quite narrow and tend to be congested, and the average speed is high, making the roads dangerous and not suitable if you want to enjoy the scenery. Ireland also has a wide network of charming little rural roads that are perfect for crossing the country. The only disadvantage of these roads is that (true to Irish custom) they are designed to take you from A to B within the shortest possible distance, which means that many roads will take you across steep hills and deep valleys. As a route planner, my task is to avoid these types of inconveniences and – with a few exceptions – I have succeeded, which means you can now complete this tour of Ireland under virtually any condition. And even if you are forced to slog uphill for a while, you should always remember that things could be significantly worse.

While Ireland is not a flat country and relatively high hilltops are visible in most areas, the highest peak you will find on this route from Belfast to Dublin is 300 metres – it is only when you take the route through Dingle or the Wicklow Mountains that you will encounter higher altitudes. For this route, I alternated routes through mountainous areas with smoother trails, which allows you to use your physical strength more efficiently.

This route will take you across virtually all of Ireland's highlights; only Giant's Causeway in the North East of the country and Donegal in the North West are excluded, since a proper route through those areas is quite a wild ride and not suitable for all cyclists.

This route isn't completely circular as it doesn't include Dublin to Belfast. While there are certainly some sights worth seeing on the route between Dublin and Belfast, most of this trail is not appealing enough to spend several days exploring it by bicycle. Indeed, there are excellent train and bus connections serving this area.

With the exception of Belfast, Dublin, Cork and – to a lesser extent –

Galway, Ireland is a very sparsely populated country. While there are certainly plenty of amenities and facilities in the more touristy areas, in some of the more rural areas arranging accommodation and shopping for food may take a little planning. A B&B may be easier to find than a shop in these areas, but both the guide and the map indicate all facilities and amenities.

Season, climate, accommodation, food and preparation

The average temperatures in Ireland hover between 6 degrees Celsius in January and 16 degrees during the summer months. It hardly ever snows or freezes, but in the summer there are usually a couple of warm days with temperatures of up to 24 degrees – it rarely gets much warmer than that. The best time of year for a cycling tour is May to September. Statistically speaking, April is the driest month countrywide, while June is the driest month in the south; however, don't be mistaken: you may well find yourself taking cover from the rain at any time of year.

People simply let it come down and ignore it by having a cup of hot tea or a pint of Guinness. It tends to rain more often in the West, and when it does they are usually showers: a short, heavy downpour that is suddenly interrupted by bright, sunny spells, with just a hint of dampness remaining. The driest part of the country is the south east, making it excellent for cycling from April through September.

Although you are sure to stay warm as long as you keep moving, you need to be well prepared for chillier temperatures during the cooler months. Particularly when you stop to admire the view, the cool wind can go straight through your clothing. You should therefore make sure that you always pack enough windproof clothes to prevent hypothermia. Exposure to low temperatures can be dangerous, especially in areas where there are few places that provide shelter.

On some routes, there can be great distances between shops, so if you find yourself suddenly peckish or if your bike breaks down, you must make sure you have plenty of food and drink with you. Just pack plenty of bananas, energy bars and/or chocolate to keep you going, and regularly refill your water bottle — drinking tap water is perfectly safe throughout Ireland.

The quality of the food in Ireland is excellent. The traditional full Irish breakfast is extremely filling, and, although the combo of eggs, bacon, sausages, black pudding and beans is hardly healthy fare, it is sure to keep you going well past noon. A healthier alternative is to start the day with cereal or toast with butter and jam. At B&Bs, it is quite common to be offered porridge (traditional Irish oatmeal) in the morning.

Hot meals are served in almost every pub. Portions tend to be big, and the Irish like their meat and potatoes, although the selection of fish and seafood is excellent as well, the long coastline being home to plenty of mussels and oysters. Vegetarians will find something to their liking in most pubs and restaurants, although the selection tends to be a bit more limited in very rural areas. A common sight are the signs advertising carvery lunches: in these pubs the person behind the counter will make you up a plate of meat, potatoes and vegetables. The portions are generous and you usually get pretty good value for money.

All medium-sized Irish cities and towns have pizzerias, kebab joints, Chinese takeaways and similar fast-food places, ensuring you can find a decent place to eat even if you just want to have a small bite in the evening. Fish and chips are available from local 'chippers', should that strike your fancy.

Ireland offers a large variety of accommodation. For those who prefer camping, the distances between campsites are sometimes inconvenient, and in some areas, such as Northern and Eastern Ireland, campsites are extremely scarce full stop. However, there are plenty of Bed & Breakfasts throughout the country, with prices ranging from highly affordable in the countryside to more expensive in the cities and near popular tourist sites. You will also find luxury B&Bs, which are housed in country estates – I have not distinguished between these various types in this guide.

There are also a large number of hostels throughout Ireland, whose prices range somewhere between campsites and B&Bs. I have not listed hostels and youth hostels separately in this guide, as the setup and rules of these types of accommodation tend to be similar.

In the larger towns and near the most scenic areas along the route you will also find hotels, with prices, as before, varying based on location and the amenities provided. Prices in Ireland rose sharply during the economic boom of recent years, but now that the economy has taken a turn for the

worse, prices have dropped as well. That is to say, they may not have changed in the official guides, but once you check in at the front desk you'll be able to secure a better rate.

Along with the categories listed above, there are also several guesthouses and pubs that have rooms available – I have included this type of accommodation under B&Bs. All the symbols are indicated on their location on the map whenever possible; however, if there are multiple amenities and facilities for a specific category, a symbol is only included next to the name of the town, for the sake of legibility. For some B&Bs in rural areas we were able to track down the location, but not the telephone number – these B&Bs are included as a symbol only.

One of the most enjoyable ways to end the day (or start the evening) is with a good glass of whiskey. There are five major brands: Jameson, Bushmills, Tullamore Dew, Powers and Paddys. There are also a large number of more exclusive malt whiskeys, which, while costing a bit more, are also ultimately more satisfying. If you don't really care for spirits, the stouts Guinness and Murphy's are excellent as well. Some say they taste of Ireland itself, and you'll find that the second glass always tastes better than the first.

Transport

The fastest way to travel to Ireland is by aeroplane. A low-cost company like Easyjet flies direct to Belfast from several airports in the UK and Europe, while Aer Lingus flies to Dublin and Cork. Ryanair operates flights from Dublin to more than 50 European destinations, as well as from Britain to Belfast. From Belfast Airport, it is best to travel by bus to the city centre or first cycle to Antrim (9 kilometres) and from there take the train to Belfast. I would not recommend cycling along the main road to Belfast (30 kilometres). However, it is possible to cycle from Dublin Airport to the city; the route is indicated for cyclists as well.

Alternatively, if you don't like flying there's always the boat and train, via either England or France. From Stranraer you can catch a boat to Belfast seven times a day, with a total journey time of three hours. You can also take the ferry from Holyhead in Wales to Dublin, or from Fishguard to Rosslare. Bear in mind, however, that you will need to make several transfers with your bike, which can be a hassle. Another alternative is to sail to Cork from the French town of Cherbourg (in Normandy).

Once you've arrived in Ireland, you can take your bike on the train with you as well as on the Bus Eireann buses, provided there is enough space. The only modes of transport on which you are not permitted to bring your bicycle are the trains between Dublin and Sligo, the DART (the train that runs from Bray to Howth and back along the Dublin coast) and Dublin Bus.

The entire tour, half, or the other way around?

This route runs from Belfast to Dublin, making it counter-clockwise. The route is designed this way because it allows you to start slowly, with a 25-kilometre bicycle path along the green banks of the Lagan. This will also allow those accustomed to cycling on the right-hand side of the road to to get used to cycling on the left. Once you have completed this route, the climb from the south up the Wicklow Mountains will be a breeze, followed by a quick descent to Dublin. If you did the tour the other way around, starting out in Dublin, you would find those first few kilometres quite challenging, and besides, ending your journey in Dublin feels like something of a victory. These few exceptions notwithstanding, this route is also perfectly manageable if you start in the other direction.

Not all cyclists will be willing or able to complete the entire route: those who don't want to cycle the whole distance can take the train from Dublin to Westport and from there start the route through Connemara. Alternatively, Galway and Tralee are excellent locations to either continue or finish the route. If you don't want to spend more than a week cycling you may want to consider flying to Cork and from there cycle to Dublin and back. The trail is easy and full of variety, with beautiful, gentle scenery, and will take you through the driest and warmest part of the country, with the wind at your back.

ULSTER

Until recently, Belfast was a fast-growing city with a dynamic city centre and a bustling nightlife. After the Troubles, the city centre was revitalised, which means that, alongside the ancient monuments, you will now find many pleasant shopping streets lined with cafés and restaurants. Near to the start of the route you will find Ireland's oldest indoor market, the Saint George's Market. Right next door is the Waterfront Hall, a theatre with a striking dome, which provides a stunning view over Belfast.

Both the Catholic and the Protestant neighbourhoods still have their share of murals, but a different Belfast is clearly emerging, one that is focused on a more positive attitude to life. One of the new additions is the construction of a cycle track through the Lagan Valley. This bicycle route starts out near Belfast's main train station (see the city map) and follows this path across a distance of 25 kilometres through a lush green landscape. Apart from the odd runner and fellow cyclists, you will not really notice the presence of the city here, and as you head out farther the roads across the valley also disappear and you will already be out of the city.

At the end of the cycle track, the road (which features signs) continues into the gently rolling farmland between the hills and Lough Neagh. The route will then take you back to the more park-like area around Craigavon, and from there to the buildings and town centre of Portadown. I tried to cycle a little closer to the lake, but unfortunately there were no bridges across the river before Portadown.

This latter town is a small provincial city with a pleasant town centre. It, too, saw its share of violent attacks during the Troubles, and people now seem eager to put the past behind them. You won't come across any shops along this route until after 40 kilometres, so be sure to stock up on food and drink while you're here. As you leave Portadown, you will cycle through a very small strip of one of the more impoverished neighbourhoods; once you have passed through this area, you will find yourself back in the gentle green land around the lake. The route along the lake is not long, but that's not really a problem as it means you will only have to deal with midges for so long. While these little insects don't sting, they can be annoying. The route then leads into the hills, towards the Sperrin Mountains. The scenery is even more gorgeous here. Once you have passed Cookstown, it will be another 40 kilometres before you come across any shops. The landscape also becomes steeper here – you can tell this is the start of the Sperrin Mountains.

The route through the valley will initially lead you through more woodland and along an old watermill. The panoramas become wider and the tops of the hills only feature rough vegetation.

Although you won't be able to climb too high here, the route does have a few short, challenging ascents. Gortin is a charming little town (with a shop) at the foot of the hill. It is home to the Gortin Glen Forest Park, a beautiful, spacious wooded area. The official route spirals here, but you can also ascend directly across the main road. The climb is quite easy (if you've taken a break beforehand) and the route that follows, through the forest, is spectacular. On the other side you will head down into the stunning landscape. Down in the valley (not directly along the route) is the Ulster American Folk

Park, where visitors can discover how people used to live in this area in dire poverty and how these Scotch-Irish emigrants (as they became known) were compelled to build a new life in the United States. I thought the park was a fascinating experience, particularly because of the large numbers of American visitors who come there to discover their roots. To get to the Ulster American Folk Park, you need to cross the river, which you can only do three kilometres north or three kilometres south of the park. The official bicycle route already makes a detour here of several kilometres, and this adds even more to the distance. But it's worth it, as it makes for a highly educational journey.

Omagh is another pleasant provincial town that offers all modern conveniences. Traditionally a relatively sleepy town, Omagh suddenly made world headlines in August 1998, when a bloody bomb attack by the Real IRA killed twenty-nine people, including a large number of children. It was one of the last attacks before peace finally came to Northern Ireland. En route from Omagh to Enniskillen, you will pass through gently rolling land alternated with small wooded areas. Even though this is traditional farmland, the farms are actually few and far between.

Enniskillen, the capital of County Fermanagh, is a charming little town. A major fishing spot, the town is also a popular destination for boats, which sail across the Lower Lough Erne southward to the River Shannon in the Republic of Ireland. The town's history is marked by conflict, and the names of both the Royal Inniskilling Fusiliers and the lesser-known Inniskilling Dragoon Guards are derived from the town's name. You will have the opportunity to discover more about the town's history in the 15th-century castle.

Enniskillen is also famous for being the birthplace of two of Ireland's greatest writers, Oscar Wilde and Samuel Beckett.

Located just east of Enniskillen is Castle Coole. Set in a 1,200-acre wooden estate, this neo-classical Georgian mansion gives the area a 'cool' quality, as it were, and not only because of its name.
For all its acknowledged beauty, the mansion remains somewhat aloof, which is why I think the more southern Florence Court is a lot more beautiful. This is no doubt to do with the landscape, as once you've passed Enniskillen the scenery becomes much more interesting. The vegetation becomes denser, and you gradually ascend to the foot of the hills in the south. The route doesn't require you to climb too high, but the hills do get more rugged as you ascend. The clouds, too, which drift in from the west, are often separated by the mountains, which means you see both dark skies and bright sunlight across the horizon. To me, that's the most vivid representation of Ireland's beauty.

Just before you get to the hill the route bends to the right, but to visit Florence Court you need to take a turn to the left (this is indicated on the signs). You are now actually ascending through the park, before the park landscape opens up, and the elegant estate perched on top becomes visible. The estate, which was built by the Counts of Enniskillen, features a lavishly-decorated interior with several beautiful paintings. To continue with the trail after visiting Florence Court

1 From East Bridge Street, above the station, down to bike path. Follow bike path through the valley.

1 Follow cycling route 9.

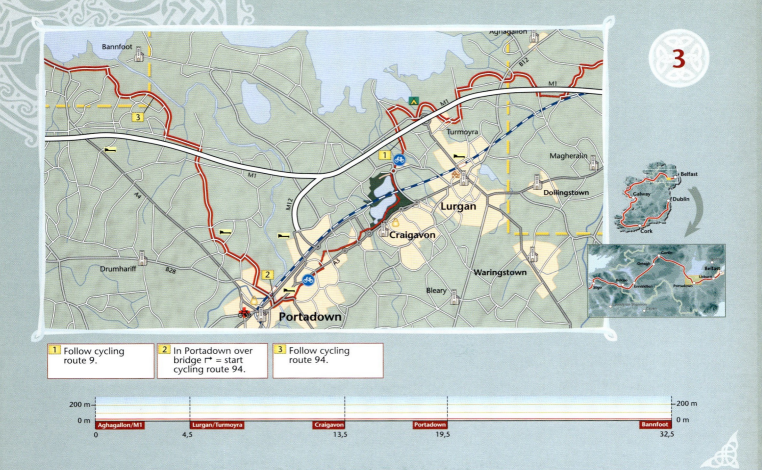

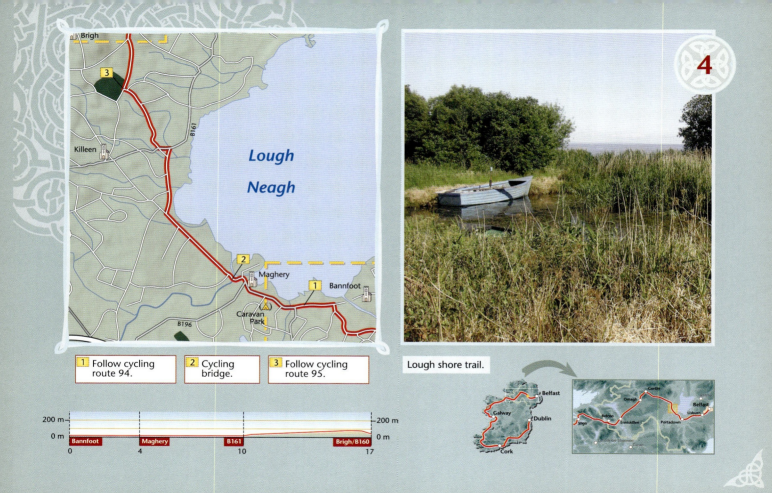

Lough shore trail.

1	Follow cycling route 94.
2	Cycling bridge.
3	Follow cycling route 95.

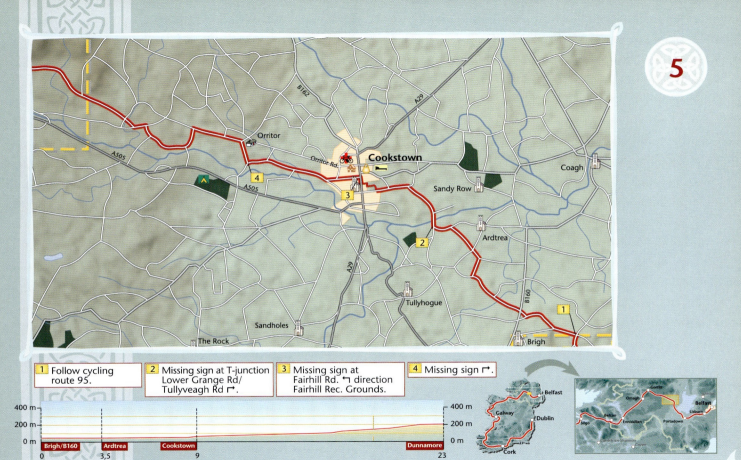

Cycling path along the Lagan

Sperrin Mountains

Ulster Cows

Ulster American Folk Park

FLORENCE COURT ... **AND THE HILLS BEHIND**

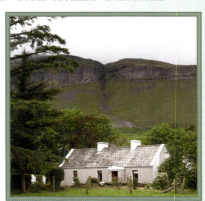

FUCHSIA **AT THE FOOT OF BENBULBEN**

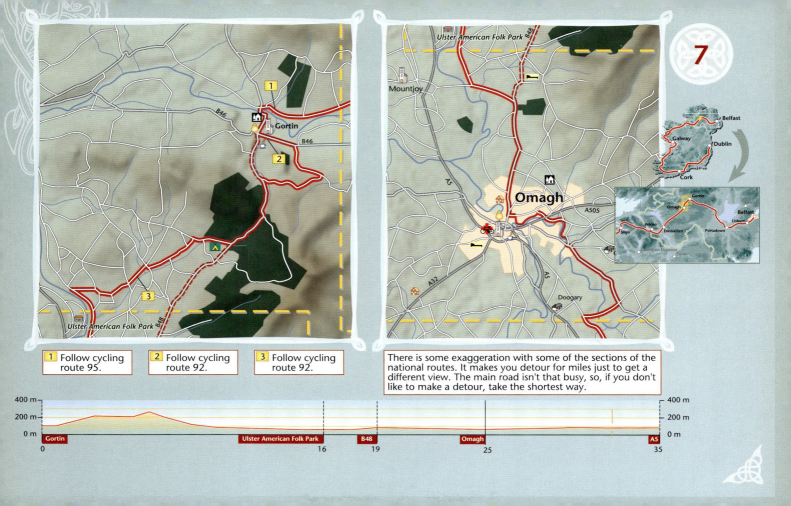

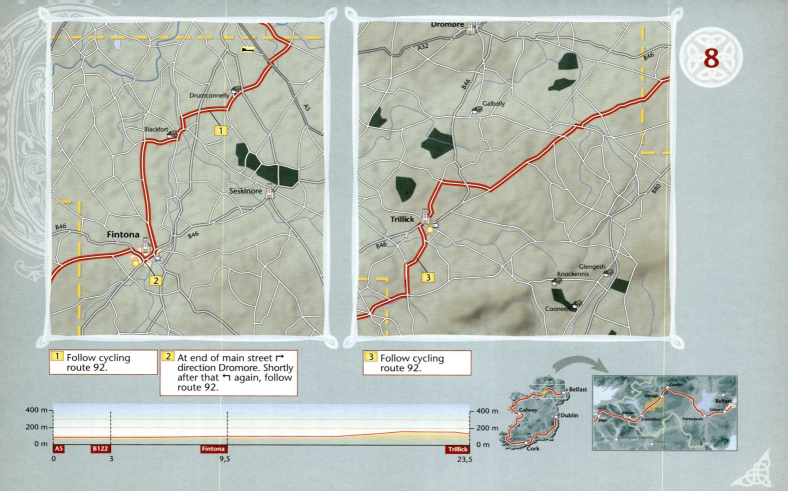

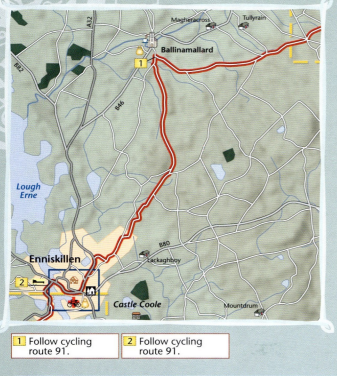

| 1 | Follow cycling route 91. | 2 | Follow cycling route 91. |

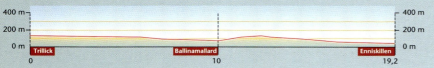

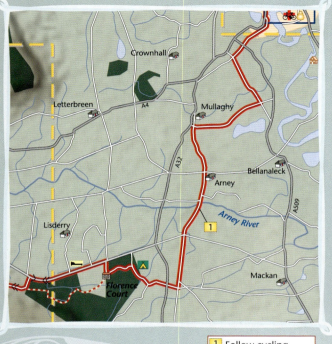

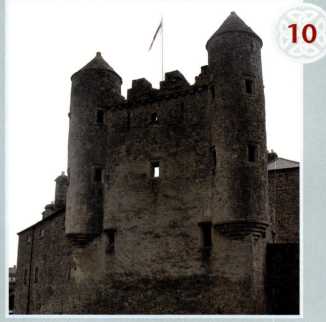

10

1 Follow cycling route 91.

Enniskillen Castle.

Enniskillen — Florence Court — 16,7

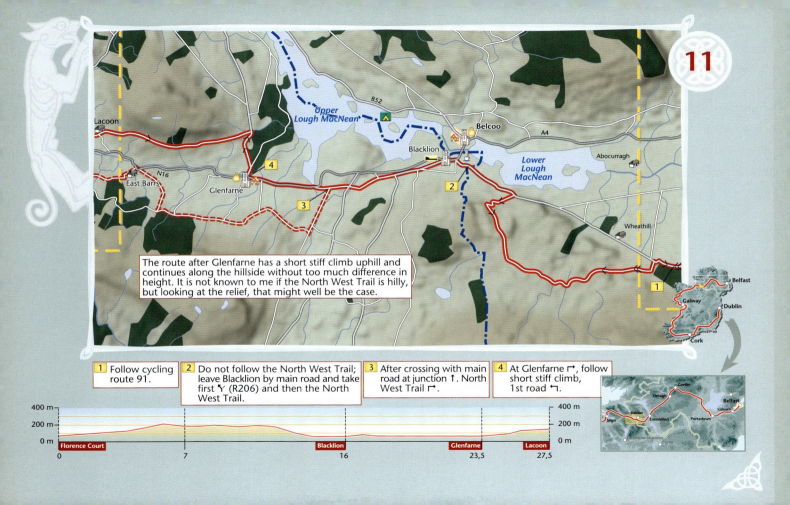

1 ↑ over main road.

2 Angle Y on to N16.

3 In Manorhamilton through town centre. At crossroads after centre ↑. 1st road ↰ direction Lurganboy. Before roundabout ↰ di. Lurganboy. Continue climbing to highest point in Lurganboy, then ↱.

4 Continue following path ↑ along hillside.

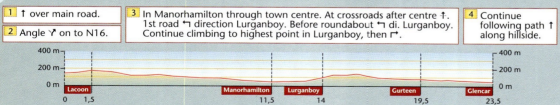

you first need to return to the lower road. It is only after several kilometres that the route actually turns into the hills, on the left side. Although you will need to keep pedalling for a while, you'll find that the view more than makes up for it. If the weather is particularly miserable, just continue cycling down below, since you'll still want to catch something of the scenery.

The mini-tour of the hills is only several kilometres, and the place where the route descends again marks the entrance of the Marble Arch Caves, which are open to visitors. Shortly after, at Blacklion, you will cross the border to the Republic of Ireland virtually unnoticed. The currency changes here from sterling to euro; if you still have some sterling left in your pockets, just head across the bridge to Belcoo in Northern Ireland to get yourself something to eat and drink.

From Blacklion, the route runs westward. A new route has been planned (the Northwest Trail), which differs from the route I devised myself. The trail up to Manorhamilton may well be superior to my own route, but it certainly seems longer. Farther ahead, between Manorhamilton and Sligo, the route of the North West Trail led across a path on a hill that was so steep that you had to carry your bike, bags and all, in order to cross it. It seems as though some local route planners gear their routes to a completely different type of cyclist.

In order to avoid the traffic, the route also runs across a hill ridge that offers outstanding views over the valley. Manorhamilton has a lovely, peaceful atmosphere, its high street decorated with bright colours. The town has cafés, restaurants and enough shops to stock up if needed. After Manorhamilton, you will once again make your way up before the gradual descent towards the sea. That mountain looming before you is the imposing Benbulben: it was famously a source of inspiration to the poet William Butler Yeats, who is buried at the foot of the mountain. Before you get there,

you will first pass Lake Glencar. Right after you take off, you can turn to the right, through a gate and across a small path to Glencar Falls. Since there was no one around when I was there, I went by bike, but even if you just walk across it is well worth it. Glencar Falls is a beautiful waterfall that comes gushing down from on high. Be sure not to miss it!

The path along the lake is flat and bends down to Benbulben on the way to Drumcliff. If you would like to visit Yeats' grave you will need to go to the cemetery, but the route actually turns left before you get there. Once you've passed Rathcormack, you cross the main road and head up the hill once again in order to descend to narrow paths, towards the sea which you'll see glistening in the distance. Just before you get to Sligo, you cross the road through sludges and salt meadows. After you've passed the first residential neighbourhoods along the main road, take the exit to Sligo's pretty historical city centre.

ACCOMMODATION

Telephone numbers in Northern Ireland have the country prefix 0044.

Map 2
Lisburn
  Hotel the Ballymac, 7 Rock Road, ph: (0)28 9264 8313
  B&B Down Royal House, 18 Cockhill Road, Maze, ph: (0)28 9262 2179
  B&B Knockeen Lodge, 4 Limehill Road, ph: (0)28 9266 5593
  B&B Victoria Boarding House, 1 Victoria Crescent, ph: (0)28 9258 3175
  B&B Hill View Farm, 35 Stoneyford Road, ph: (0)28 9264 8270
Moira
  B&B Ballycanal Manor, 2a Glenavy Road, ph: (0)28 9261 1923
  B&B Glebe House, 2 St John's Park, ph: (0)28 9261 9553

Map 3

Lurgan

    Ashburn Hotel, 61 William Street, ph: (0)28 3832 5711

    B&B Derry Lodge, 7 Derrylodge Manor, ph: (0)28 3832 9577

    Kinnego Marina Caravan Park, ph: (0)28 3832 7573

Portadown

    Bannview B&B, 60 Portmore Street, ph: (0)28 3833 6666

    B&B By the Ways, 37 Derryvore Lane, ph: (0)28 3833 4625

    B&B Redbrick Country House, Corbrackey Lane, ph: (0)28 3833 5268

Map 5

Cookstown

    Glenavon House Hotel, 52 Drum Road, ph: (0)28 8676 4949

    Royal Hotel, 64-72 Coagh Street, ph: (0)28 8676 2224

    Greenvale Hotel, 57 Drum Road, ph: (0)28 8676 2243

    B&B Belfast House, 3 Orritor Street, ph: (0)28 8676 9759

    B&B Manorview, 26 Upper Kildress Road, ph: (0)28 8676 1124

    Camping Drum Manor Forest Park, Drum Road, ph: (0)28 8775 9311 or (0)28 8676 2774 Contact: Forest Rangers

Map 7

Gortin

    Hostel Gortin, 62 Main Street, ph: (0)28 8164 8346

On the route 3 mile (±5km) before Omagh:

    B&B Rest. The Brasserie, 1 Glen Park Road, ph: (0)28 8224 4804

Omagh

    Silverbirch Hotel, 5 Gortin Road, ph: (0)28 8224 2520

    B&B Arandale House, 66 Drumnakilly Road, ph: (0)28 8224 3243

    B&B Arleston House, 1 Arleston Park, ph: (0)28 8224 1719

    B&B Heron's Burn, 3,5 mile north of Omagh. 51 Gortnagarn Road, ph: (0)28 8224 0106

    B&B Twenty-Three, 23 Clontarf Drive, ph: (0)28 8224 6665

    Sperrin Cottages, Caravan and Camping Park. (open Easter - late September), 1 Lisnaharney Road, ph: (0)28 8166 2288

Map 8

    The Spirit Store Bar/B&B, Main Street, Trillick, ph: (0)28 8956 1208

    Dervaghroy House, 8 mile south of Omagh, 18 Church Road, ph: (0)28 8075 7990

Map 9

Enniskillen

    There are more than 5 hotels and B&Bs in Enniskillen. Contact TIC (Tourist Information Centre)

    Hotel Killyhevlin, Dublin Road, ph: (0)28 6632 3481

Map 11

Belcoo

    Custom's House Inn, Main Street, ph: (0)28 6638 6285

    B&B Bella Vista, Cottage Drive, ph: (0)28 6638 6469

    B&B Rockview House, ph: (0)28 6638 6534

    B&B Woodford, ph: (0)28 6638 6576

    Camping Rushin House Caravan Park, ph: (0)28 6638 6519

Telephone numbers in the Republic of Ireland have the country prefix 00 353

Blacklion
Hotel Macnean House (expensive), ph: (0)71 985 3022
B&B Olive Grove (restaurant), ph: (0)71 985 3443

Glenfarne
B&Bs Clancys Of Glenfarne, Brockagh, ph: (0)71 985 3116

Map 12
Manorhamilton
B&B Bluebell House, Clooneen, Manorhamilton, ph: (0)71 985 5384
B&B Glencar House, Glencar, ph: (0)71 985 6731

Map 13
Drumcliff
There are more than 5 B&Bs in Drumcliff.
Rathcormack
Kintogher B&B, ph: (0)71 914 1755

Map 13/14
Sligo
There are more than 5 hotels and B&Bs. For more information contact TIC.
Greenlands Camping, Rosses Point, ph: (0)71 917 7113 (open 20/3 – 15/9)
Strandhill Caravan & Camping Park, Strandhill, ph: (0)71 916 8111 (open 17/04 – 30/09)

CYCLE SHOPS/REPAIRS:

Belfast
Bikedock, 79-85 Ravenhill Rd, ph: (0)28 9073 0600 (Good shop)
James McGarvey, 16 King Street, ph: (0)28 9032 8848
Brian Kinnings Cycles, 74 Castlereagh Rd, ph: (0)28 9058 9589
McConvey Cycles (cycle hire), 83 Ormeau Road, ph: (0)28 9033 0322

Lisburn
John M. Hanna, 11-15 Chapel Hill, ph: (0)28 9267 9575
Cycle Zone, 8 Railway St, ph: (0)28 9266 2066

Portadown
Ross Raymond Cycles, 65 Bridge Street, ph: (0)28 3835 2828

Cookstown
Cookstown Cycles, 2a Molesworth Rd, ph: (0)28 8676 9667

Omagh
Caldwell Motor Factors, Dromore Rd Retail Park, ph: (0)28 8224 2731
Conway Cycles, 157 Loughmacrory Road, ph: (0)28 8076 1258

Enniskillen
Patrick McNulty & Sons, 24-26 Belmore St, ph: (0)28 6632 2423

Sligo
Gary Cycles, 5 Quay St, ph: (0)71 9145418
Cranks Bicycle Repairs, 19 The Green, Ocean Links, Strandhill, ph: (087) 9564086

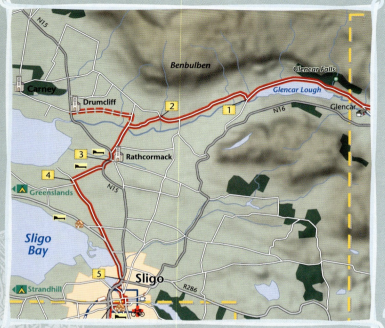

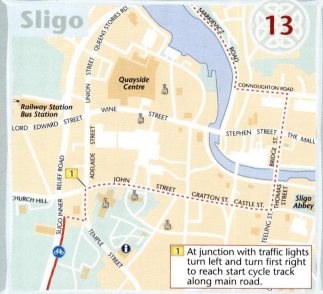

1 At junction with traffic lights turn left and turn first right to reach start cycle track along main road.

| 1 After the lake first road ↱. | 2 After 4 km ↰. At T-junction ↰. | 3 At T-junction ↰ on to main road. In the bend after climb ↱. | 4 At T-junction ↰ and afterward ↑ till traffic lights N15. | 5 At traffic lights ↱ N15 and 1st road ↰ direction centre. |

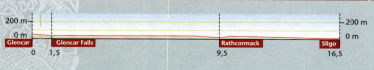

Sligo

Manorhamilton

Window view at dawn

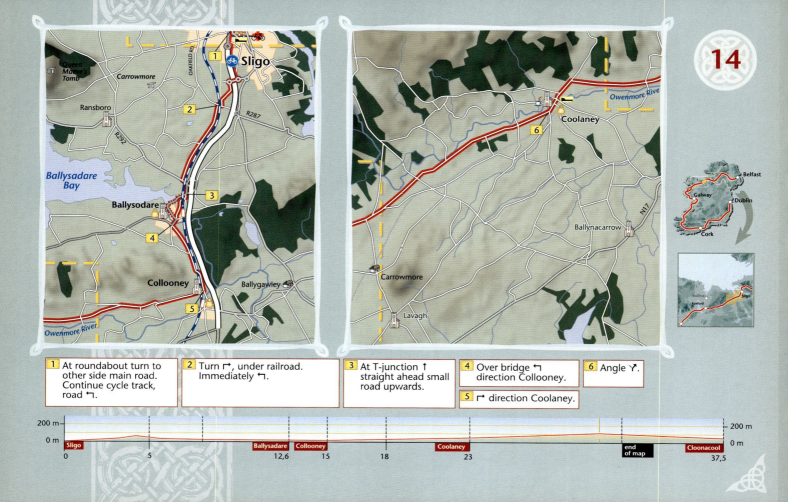

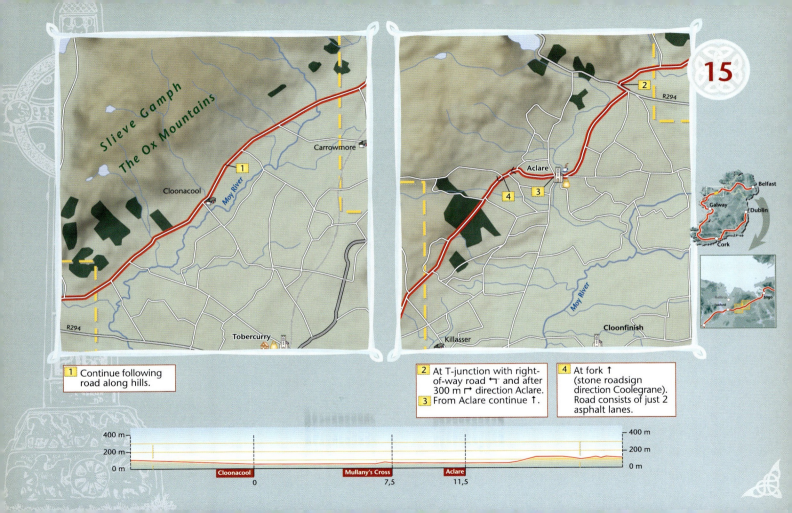

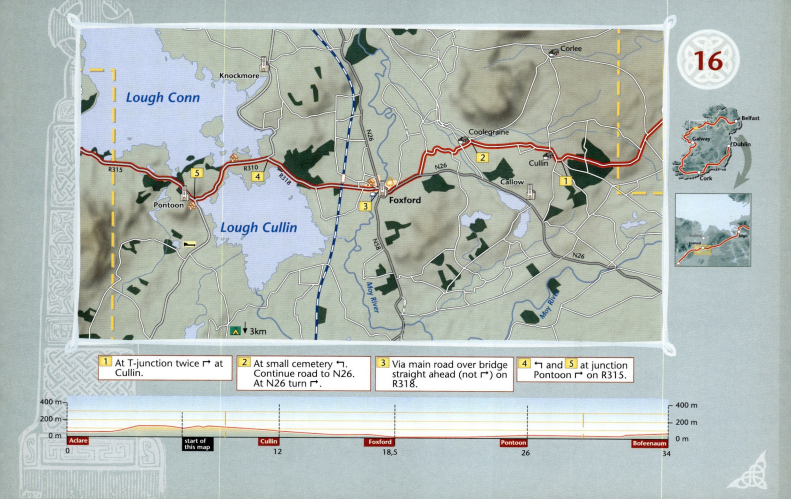

OX MOUNTAINS

LOUGH CONN NEAR PONTOON

PEATLAND

Sligo

With a population of 20,000, Sligo is the largest town in the area. The section around the Garavogue River is particularly appealing, as are several houses on the main street and the ancient abbey. The streets are lively, the food is excellent and the pubs are filled with music, making it a wonderful place to spend the night.

Once you have passed Sligo, the route leads to a strikingly beautiful, but also very empty, part of this area. The route goes along the foothills of the Ox Mountains, but once you have passed Coolaney there will be no more shops until you get to Aclare.

On your left-hand side, you'll see green, undulating land with a few scattered farms. The road is tranquil. After Aclare you get to cycle a bit higher to cut through the hill to the beautiful lakes of Lough Conn and Lough Cullin, with the view of Mount Nephin in County Mayo.

Foxford is another rest stop with shops and places to eat.

The narrow road between the two lakes runs through a forest, but the occasional open areas provide beautiful views and beaches. After passing Pontoon, you first carry on along the lake before making your way upward to the small lakes at the bottom of the mountain. At Lake Beltra you'll witness a traditional peat bog, with large black strips of excavated land and stacks of peat drying in the sun. On your left, you will see a mountain that you're going to climb before descending to what looks like a dune landscape in Westport. What you'll find here are not sand dunes exactly, but a number of low, small hills that appear to have been formed by sand deposits. Westport is a very lively and beautiful tourist town, which serves as a local centre for people visiting Connemara and Mayo. Westport is situated at the end of a railway that starts in Dublin. The town also attracts pilgrims, who come here to climb Croagh Patrick.

Accommodation

Map 14

Ballisodare
  B&B Ballincrone, Corhownagh, ph: (0)71 913 0110
  B&B Seashore, Lisduff, ph: (0)71 916 7827
  B&B The Rowans, Kilmacowen, ph: (0)71 916 7337
Collooney
  Markree Castle Hotel, ph: (0)71 916 7800
  B&B Chestnut Lodge, Old Barrack Road, ph: (0)71 916 7330
Coolaney
  B&B JJ O'Grady, Main Street, ph: (0)71 916 7211
  Mountain Inn, ph: (0)71 916 7225

Map 15

Aclare
  B&B Haggart Lodge, Lislea, ph: (0)71 918 1954

Map 16
Foxford

   Mayfly Hotel, Main Street, ph: (0)94 925 6801

   B&B Lakeland, Pontoon Road, ph: (0)94 925 6880

   B&B Woodview House, Coolcronan, ph: (0)94 925 8287

Pontoon

   Healy's Restaurant And Country House Hotel, ph: (0)94 925 6443

   Pontoon Bridge Hotel, ph: (0)94 925 6120

   Knockaglana House B&B (2km south of Pontoon), (0)94 925 6982

   Carrowkeel Camping and Caravan Park, Ballyvary, Castlebar. (6 miles south of Pontoon), ph: (0)94 903 1264 (open from Easter – 01/10)

Map 18
Murrisk

   Béal An tSáile B&B, ph: (0)98 64012

   Camping Westport, Murrisk, ph: (0)87 659 7842

Westport

   here are more than 5 hotels and B&Bs in Westport.

   For more information contract TIC (Tourist Information Centre)

   Old Mill Holiday Hostel, James Street, ph: (0)98 27045

   Parkland Caravan and Camping Park, ph: (0)98 27766

CYCLE SHOPS/REPAIRS:

Castlebar

   Bike Clinic, Springfield, ph: (0)94 902 4800

Westport

   Breheny J P & Sons, Castlebar St, ph: (0)98 25020

A TASTE OF
CONNEMARA

Legend has it that Christianity was introduced in Ireland by St Patrick. According to the myth, he was born in Dumbarton, Scotland around 390, to Roman parents. At the age of sixteen he was captured by Irish marauders and taken to Ireland, where he was enslaved and used as a shepherd. At the age of twenty-two he managed to escape and returned to Scotland. Once he arrived there, he had a vision of returning to Ireland as a missionary in order to preach the faith. He first set out for Tours in France and then to Auxerre to enrol in the seminary there and prepare for the priesthood, before being ordained as a priest in Rome.

When he returned to Ireland as a monk, he found shelter with one of the first Christians to have been converted after engaging in trade with people on the land.

He managed to get through to the tribal leaders, and legend has it that he convinced two princesses of the concept of the holy trinity by showing them the shamrock and using it to highlight the Christian belief of 'three divine persons in the one God'. For this reason, the shamrock is the symbol of Ireland, along with the harp.

Apart from preaching, St Patrick's life revolved around frequent periods of atonement, fasting and retreats in the most forbidding places. One of the places where he retreated for an extended period to pray and fast was the mountain near Westport, the present-day Croagh Patrick. Today, this mountain is one of the most important pilgrim destinations in Ireland. On the last Sunday in July, Westport is flooded by pilgrims who climb the mountain in large numbers. Many do this as a form of repentance, preferably barefoot, while others hope to be healed. The truly devout complete the last kilometre of the journey on their knees.

I have never been and never will be a pilgrim, but it is amazing to observe how a people bears its suffering. Would these deprivations make people stronger in coping with their daily lives? What kind of mentality does it take to get through the winters here?

After leaving Westport, on the way to Louisburgh, you will see the pilgrims approaching from the hamlet of Murrisk and climbing up the mountain from the broad path down below. I have explored a new route from Westport to Leenane, which is less crowded than the route through Louisburgh and at least as beautiful. Although there is a lovely bicycle path from Westport to Westport Quay, and from there, along the main road to Murrisk (the start of the pilgrim's path to Croagh Patrick), is another cycle track along the road complete with picnic spots and bike racks, traffic there is extremely busy, especially during the summer months. Another lovely route in the area is the

42 kilometre Greenway from Westport to Achill Sound, which runs, off road, along the old railway route.

Our route to Leenane runs from Westport directly southward around Croagh Patrick. The most direct route from the city centre starts out with an ultra-steep climb, which I wasn't able to manage. It is therefore better to first follow the main road down to Clifden until you have passed the old cycle track. You then take the first turn to the left and the first turn to the right. You continue straight ahead until you get to the crossing where you can turn left to Aghagower. You then head up the steep hill and continue climbing until you get to Croagh Patrick. After one kilometre, the descent to Liscarney begins. From here, you cross the main road and follow the signposted bicycle route to Killary Harbour. Halfway across the trail to Leenane, you end up at a narrow, one-kilometre pass, and if there's no wind you may be able to remain on your bike for the entire journey. The views on the other side are beautiful, and even if it's not what you're looking for,

be sure to stop by the picnic spot, and then continue for another ten metres to admire the equally impressive view there.

The route to Louisburgh also offers beautiful views over the bay and the Mayo Mountains on the other side. Louisburgh is a friendly town with a nice selection of restaurants and shops, where you can get groceries for the next stretch of the journey, which is, frankly, stunning. After Louisburgh, the route slowly leads up to the looming

mountains. The landscape becomes increasingly forbidding, almost as if you were entering *Lord of the Rings* territory. But it's actually the other way around – it was scenery such as this that inspired Tolkien. Then, from a low pass, you will have a beautiful view of a stunning mountain lake to which the road descends. The lake is wedged between two high hillsides, and with the wind always penetrating through everything, the weather here is always gusty. After the lake, the route leads down to a beautiful small forest only to continue along the flowing river, through the valley, where you'll discover the most beautiful shades of green, ranging from silver-green-grey to a bright green that's reminiscent of artificial grass.

Sheep roam free in this area. While they're not afraid of cars – they are used to them by now – they are scared to bits every time a cyclist catches them unawares.

At the lake, the shorter, less busy, trail also ends back at the route. The route leads up to Ireland's only fjord, where the small estuary reaches 20 kilometres into the land and is deep enough to accommodate large ships. Indeed, during World War II this bay was used as a safe haven for Allied ships.

The scenery here is beautiful, but it's frustrating that the stretch on which you are currently biking with the wind at your back will later need to be completed with the wind in your face (or vice versa). Near the easternmost part, the Errif river flows into the estuary, but just before that you'll see a beautiful waterfall in the stream from this route. This area is also dense with rhododendrons, which makes everything look stunning in May. You complete the final kilometres to Leenane across a slightly busier section, as that is the only road for all routes leading through Connemara.

The majority of cars you see here have Irish number plates, but many of these are driven by tourists who rented the car at the airport. As a result, people's driving conduct can be annoying, because they have a habit of suddenly stopping to take a photograph. As a cyclist, you'll sometimes need to perform acrobatics to avoid crashing into an open car door.

Leenane provides excellent accommodation in the friendly hotel of the same name en route to Clifden. Out of season the hotel is very affordable, and you will enjoy a beautiful view from the rooms on the seaside (which actually resembles a lake). From Leenane, the main route leads to Clifden and through the shortest route it runs along Kylemore Abbey and the Twelve Bens. However, there is a less busy alternative to the trail

between Leenane and Clifden, although 'less busy' is relative, since Connemara is so gorgeous that many Irish people own second homes here as well. Even on the small roads, you will regularly encounter cars. Still, it is a beautiful road along a strip of the Atlantic Coast, full of bays and the odd campsite. Once you have passed Leenane, you cycle towards Clifden and then slowly make your way upwards. After the ascent, you turn right towards Tully Cross, and from there you turn left again, to Letterfrack. This route is no longer flat: there is a steep hill, particularly from the coast to Tully Cross, and you can expect more hills when you cycle from Tully Cross to Letterfrack. You will get through these hills relatively quickly.

After passing Letterfrack, you will first encounter a steep hill that goes down, followed by a slightly less steep climb towards Clifden. When you're

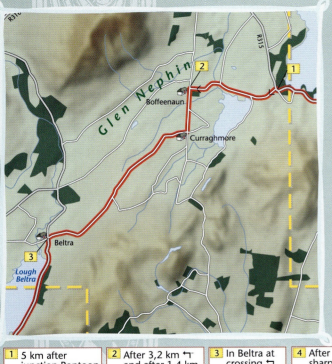

1 5 km after junction Pontoon ↰ direction Bofeenaun.	**2** After 3,2 km ↰ and after 1,4 km ↱ direction Newport.	**3** In Beltra at crossing ↰ direction Castlebar.	**4** After 4,2km in bend sharp ↰. After 700m road bends to right. Here Y. ± 1km steep climbing.	**5** Keep right and at crossing with right of way road ↑.	**6** After 700 m ↱, again after 700 m ↰.	**7** After 3,75 km ↰, after 200 m ↱.

WESTPORT

6.00 AM

6.10 AM

6.15 AM

6.20 AM

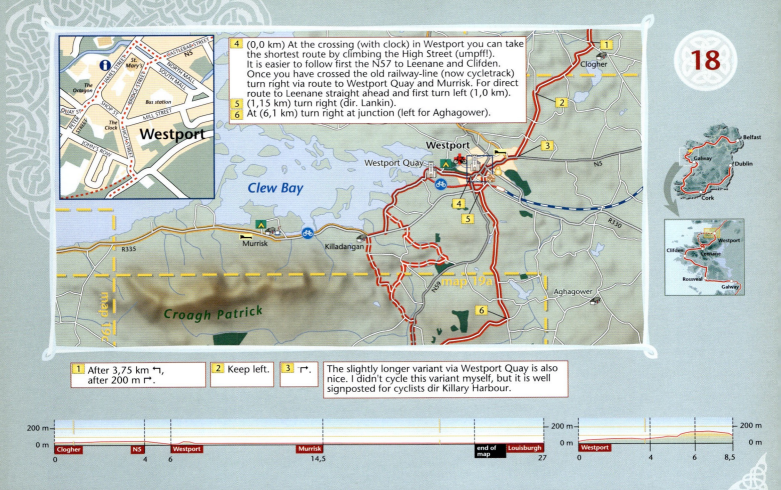

19a

1 (6,1 km) ↱, (6,3 km) climb untill (7,3 km) At 8,3 km decline.

2 (9,7 km) Liscarney. Cross main road ↑, follow signposted cycle route direction Killary Harbour.

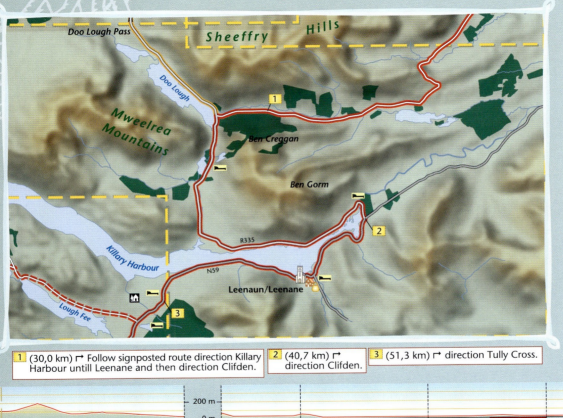

1 (30,0 km) ↪ Follow signposted route direction Killary Harbour untill Leenane and then direction Clifden.   **2** (40,7 km) ↪ direction Clifden.   **3** (51,3 km) ↪ direction Tully Cross.

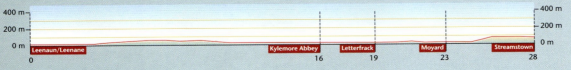

halfway across, you can turn into the famous Sky Road with its beautiful views.

If you have less time, you can also skip through part of Connemara by turning left a few kilometres after Leenane, and before Kylemore Abbey (an absolute must-see), and then cycle south behind the Twelve Bens, another beautiful route.

The first common part of the route runs along the banks of the fjord. After several kilometres, the road slowly ascends and the view of the fjord will change constantly. You will also see the open sea from here. You'll need to keep going for a while, after which the road will descend to the lake where Kylemore Abbey is located. Just before, the route bends sharply to the left. The main route runs along the lake, after which Kylemore Abbey looms up on the right. This country estate, which was built by a wealthy politician (MP) from Manchester in 1860, provided shelter to Benedictine Nuns from Belgium after WWI, who turned it into an international girls' boarding school. This school is set to close, but the nuns will continue to reside there

for the time being. The building, location and gardens all make Kylemore Abbey well worth a visit.

The route then continues to Clifden via Letterfrack. The views of the coast are stunning, and those who would like to explore more of the area should absolutely cycle down to the Sky Road.

Clifden is a delightful town and a good place to stay when visiting Connemara. When the weather's good, it is also an excellent place to enjoy some quiet time. Clifden was established by John d'Arcy in the early 19th century. He hoped to develop the region by promoting the sale of wool and sheep. The Irish famine, known as The Great Hunger (1845-1848), sadly defeated his efforts.

South of Clifden, you will find a vast area of peat land. This irregular landscape rises and falls and there are small lakes throughout the region. Large strips of peat have been extracted from the soil and left to dry. Formerly manual processes are now performed mechanically, which has had an impact on the regional economy: there is fear that the entire peat industry will disappear in the near future. It's important to preserve the unique peatland, but it may be a challenge to persuade people during an economic crisis that they should not be using cheap fuel.

The scenery in this area has an eerie quality to it. On my first visit here it was drizzling and the place was deserted, while the ponds showed no sign of life. If there is really such a thing as purgatory, this may very well be what it looks like. It was only during my second visit that the sun made an appearance and I could see the mighty Twelve Bens from a distance. Beauty doesn't always have to mean prettiness: the desolation of this landscape is beautiful in its own way.

The route through the peat land is briefly interrupted when you cycle along the creek near Cashel. This is another town where you can stop for something to eat and drink. This area of Connemara is part of the Gaeltacht, where Irish is the main language. All road signs and most of the information signs are in Irish only, which sometimes causes confusion as to what direction to take.

At the end of the peat land you will find yourself on the R340 motorway, after which you'll continue along the creeks again.
Our notion of the sea is limited: when you look out onto the water near Leenane the sea resembles a lake, and amid all these small green islands you could easily mistake the sea for random ponds. You've got quite a few kilometres ahead of you when you're near Rossaveal Harbour (Irish name: *Ros a' Mhíl*). The route splits just before Rossaveal. A part of the route runs across the landscape to Galway and from there to The Burren.

Galway is a lively, fun student town with plenty of nightlife opportunities. After passing Galway Bay, the route continues through the barren landscape of The Burren. On the way, you will pass dolmens and stone forts that are more than 2,000 years old.

The other stretch of the route will take you to the Aran Islands by boat. Known for their pristine ruggedness and Irish-speaking population, these are fascinating islands where people have literally carved out an existence by building stone walls with their hands and conquered the rough natural environment. The boat tour from Rossaveal to the largest island, Inis Mór (Inishmore), is quite enjoyable, especially when the weather is good. The tour across from Inis Mór to Doolin requires a little fearlessness. I made the journey when the weather was rough and I've never in my life been as relieved to set foot on land again. In calmer weather, you can get there by sea, from the Cliffs of Moher. However, you will need to decide in advance what route to take.

About three boats a day sail from Rossaveal to Inis Mór. From a distance, you will see the ruins of a stone fort called Dún Aengus, on top of the hill above the island. The village of Kilronan is located near the harbour – you will find all the facilities you need here. Beware that this place is far from

21

1. In centre follow Clifden (Main Street, Bridge Street) R341 direction Roundstone.
2. In Ballinaboy at junction ↰.
3. ↑ via main road R341, after 1,7 km ↱ R342 direction Cashel.

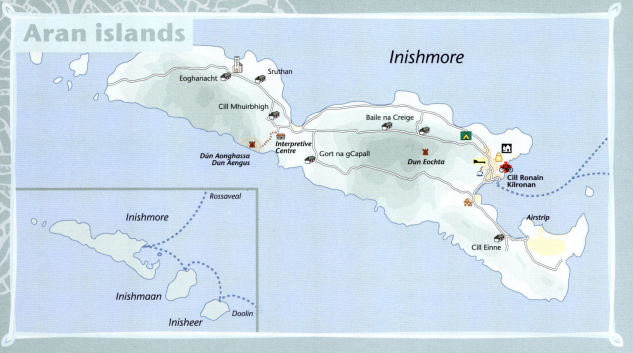

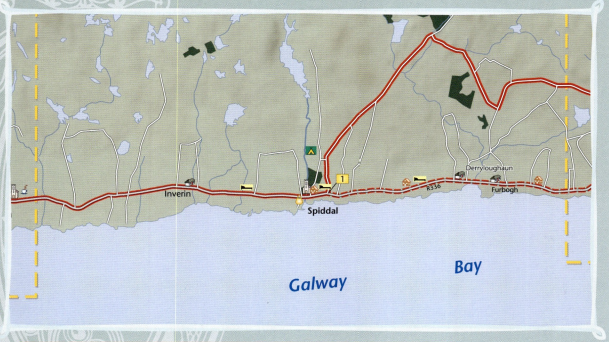

1. Turn ↰ at the Spar shop. After 7,3 km turn ↱, hill up, hill down and after 3,4 km turn ↰ and then follow the road all the way to Galway (becomes Rahoon Road).

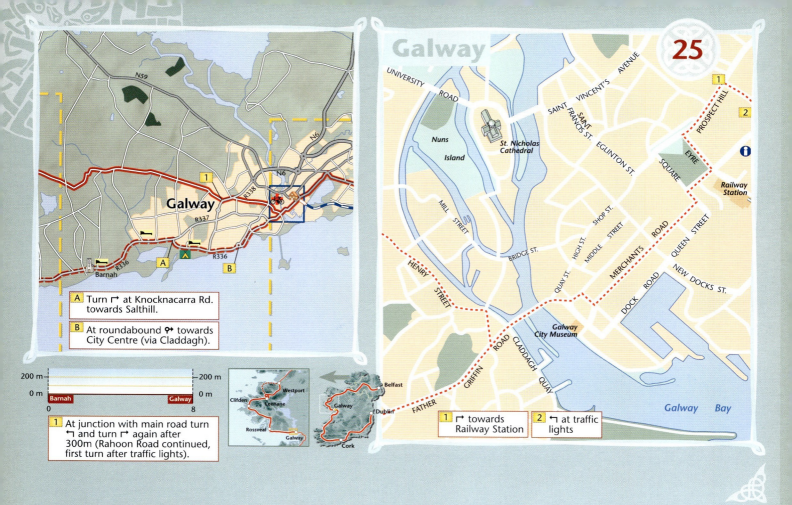

deserted – in the summer the island attracts many day-trippers who rent a bicycle to explore the island. However, there are never more bicycles than the ferry can handle, so there will still be plenty of space on the island. There are very few cars on the island, which makes it all the more startling when you do see one.

These islands were already inhabited during prehistoric times – as hard as it is to imagine, because it would have been impossible to grow anything. By stacking stones, people created enclosed plots of land, and they mixed layers of manure and seaweed to create fertile soil. Over the course of the centuries, they also used this method to create small plots of land for the livestock. You won't find any gates here; occasionally you'll come across a herd of cows grazing on a plot of enclosed land. When moving the animals to another plot of land, the locals simply break down the wall again, since they are only stones, after all.

The most interesting sight on the island is Dún Aengus, which is perched

on top of a 70-metre-high cliff. The fort consists of three rings that are open only on the sea side. The cliff runs straight down here, and no gate has been installed. You should make sure not to walk too close to the edge – in the past several tourists have fallen to their death here due to the hard wind or simple curiosity. There are three roads that run across the island between Kilronan and the fort. The road along the north coast will take you along several seal colonies. You will have to complete the last part from the fort to the visitors' centre on foot (this will take twenty minutes).

You wonder what people were thinking when they moved to these islands back in ancient times. They used little wooden boats for fishing, covered with tarred canvas. Out on the rough sea, this could be fairly risky, but all told, life on these islands may have been safer than on the land. These were tough times all over. It is well documented that many pilgrims also settled on these islands, due to their remoteness and the challenge of surviving there. The ruins of an ancient abbey are scattered all over the place.

The other two islands are less touristy. I didn't actually visit these islands, but by all accounts Inisheer has a very authentic atmosphere, which is not really true anymore for Inis Mór.

You can purchase tickets for the ferry to Doolin aboard the ferry. The price is around 10 euros; note that this is not the exact price. The shipmates will lift your bike onto the ferry and fasten it, which means you must remove your baggage first. The boat is not large, and if you are prone to seasickness I recommend that you remain on deck, sit tight, and hang on to your luggage. When the waves are high you will get splashed and the water will get between your feet. However, as long as you don't see any crew members jumping off the boat in a panic, there's no reason for you to do so either.

Once you have made it to Doolin, you will probably be ready for a drink. You're in luck, because the pubs in Doolin are known for traditional Irish music performances. You will almost always find musicians here who will dazzle you. Doolin is also the place from which to get a closer look at the Cliffs of Moher. The view is stunning, though bear in mind that this is one of Ireland's busiest tourist spots, with around one million visitors per year. There is a charge to enter the Visitor Centre. Note: it's a bit of a hike to get to the ticket office.

From Doolin, the main route leads to Lisdoonvarna, the capital of The Burren. Lisdoonvarna is a spa town, with mineral springs that help relieve all manner of ailments. The town is also home to a traditional matchmaking festival for farmers looking for a wife. This month-long festival is held each September, and the pub opening hours are extended during that time, allowing potential mates to get acquainted.

Accommodation

Map 18
Westport

There are more than 5 hotels and B&Bs in Westport. For more information you can contact or visit the TIC (Tourist Information Centre).

Old Mill Holiday Hostel, James Street, ph: (0)98 27045

Parkland Caravan and Camping Park, ph: (0)98 27766

Map 19
Louisburgh

The West View Hotel, Chapel Street, ph: (0)98 66140

There are more than 5 B&Bs.

Leenane

Leenane Hotel, ph: (0)95 42249, great night's sleep

Delphi Mountain Resort, ph: (0)95 42208

There are more than 5 B&Bs in Leenane

Map 20
Letterfrack

Rosleague Manor Hotel, ph: (0)95 41101

Letterfrack Lodge Hostel, ph: (0)95 41222

Old Monastery Hostel, ph: (0)95 41132

B&B Dooneen Lodge, Barnaderg Bay, ph: (0)95 41060

Map 21
Clifden

There are more than 5 hotels and B&Bs. For more information, please contact the TIC.

Ben Lettery Youth Hostel, near Recess, ph: (0)95 51136 (rather far)

Brookside Holiday Hostel, ph: (0)95 21812

Clifden Town Hostel, ph: (0)95 21076

Shanaheever Campsite, Westport Road, ph: (0)95 22150

Map 21/22
Cashel

Cashel House Hotel, ph: (0)95 31001

Zetland Country House Hotel, ph: (0)95 31111

Rossroe Lodge B&B, ph: (0)95 31928

Map 23
Rossaveal

B&B Hernon's, ph: (0)91 572158

Carraroe

An Doilin Hotel, Boharbee, ph: (0)91 595169

Carraroe Hotel, Ostán Cheathru Rua, ph: (0)91 595116

B&B Carraroe House, ph: (0)91 595188

B&B Donoghue's, ph: (0)91 595174

B&B Leannafion, Coral Beach Road, ph: (0)91 595159

Cycle shops/repairs:

Clifden

JM Mannion Bicycle Hire, Bridge Street, ph: (0)95 21160

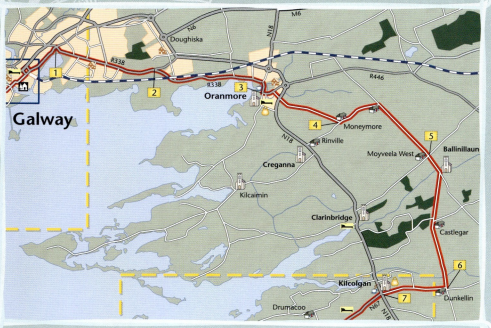

Dunguaire Castle.

26

1 At Crossing ↰ R338.	
2 After 3,6 km at junction with traffic lights ↱ R338 Follow Coast Road Oranmore.	
3 At junction ↰ upwards with the bend, after 300m ↱ (stone street name), goes over in Moneymore Road, cross Main road.	
4 At T-junction ↰. After 1,6km T-junction ↱.	
5 Continue over crossroads, after 750m angle ↱.	
6 At right of way road ↱.	
7 ↱ N67 direction Kinvara.	

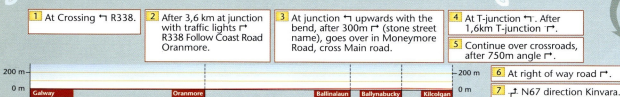

Into The Burren

Ennistymon

Kilfenora

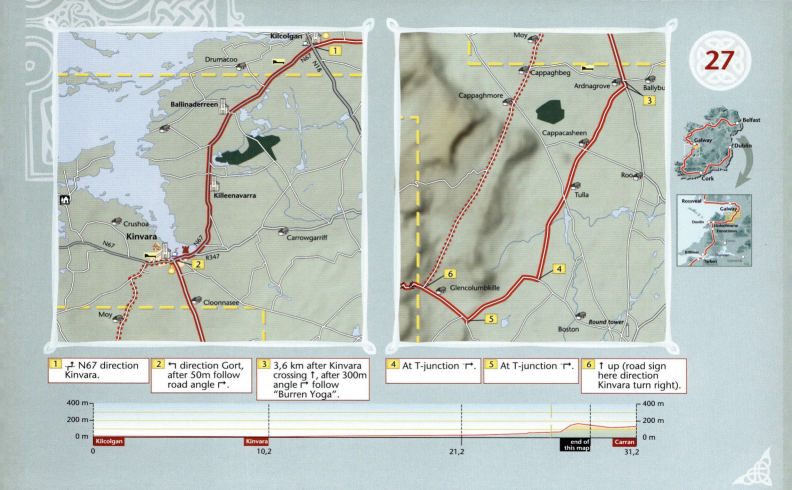

To The Burren

The road leads along the Galway Bay coast, and in clear weather you will see the Burren mountains looming in the distance. A nearby town that's good for shopping is Spiddal, where students can also enrol in Irish language classes. The centre of the village features a lovely pub and restaurant on the right that offers outdoor seating in the back on sunny days. Unfortunately, the road from here to Galway will only get busier, but this is really the only practical way to get to the city.

The capital of the West of Ireland, Galway is also the fastest-growing city in Europe. The city originated near a bridge across the River Corrib and was settled by the Anglo-Normans back in the 13th century. A century later, the city had also become a trading post between the region and Spain. Spanish merchants even had their own district in the town, the remains of which are still visible in the Spanish Arch.

The residents of the enclosed town felt they had more in common with the English than the Irish, but it so happened that they made a series of unfortunate choices.

Having chosen to join the Catholic Church, they were conquered by Cromwell's troops in 1651, after which the town was almost entirely deserted. Forty years later, history repeated itself when the population chose the side of the Catholic King James II. The town was later conquered by William of Orange.

The town fell into decay over the centuries, until it received a tremendous boost during the economic boom of the past two decades. Nowadays, it is especially popular with young people, who come here to attend university and embrace the nightlife. When you visit, you should take a walk around the car-free city centre, where you'll find a host of restaurants, cheap eats, cafés and shops. You may also find it useful to know that the man at the local bicycle shop was extremely helpful.

Until you get to Oranmore, your only real option is to take the main road, although you will be able to use the cycle track for much of the route, and the verge is certainly wide enough. Once you've passed Oranmore, the route diverges from the main road. The road is very busy and quite narrow in places, making it somewhat dangerous. The detour will take you across quiet roads to the countryside outside Galway.

From Kilcolgan to Kinvara, the route follows the main road again. Traffic is usually not too heavy here, but the landscape is not really exceptional at this stage of the trail.

Kinvara Castle is the first thing you'll see when you return to the bay. Then there's Dunguaire Castle, which was built around 1500 and has a tower that offers a wonderful view over the bay.

After this point, the route will take you into The Burren, but first it will lead you to the foot of the mountains (the land seems flat here, but don't be fooled). From this side, you should be prepared for an uphill ride – and when in a low gear you can quite easily climb up. This is nothing at all like an Alpine pass. The scenery here is rugged and beautiful. I had been told beforehand that the scenery in The Burren was eerie, and that I would find its desolation troubling. It is no wonder that Cromwell said about this area: 'There's not a tree to hang a man, water to drown a man, nor earth to bury a man.' However, that was many years before the invention of fertiliser and the start of the economic boom. In the valley you'll find well-fed cows grazing away in green pastures, and there are new, white stone farms amid the green scrubs.

This is a limestone area with subterranean rivers and stalagmite caves. There are entire stretches where you'll find only stone and shrubs, just like in the South of France, where the only vegetation is prickly bushes. But unlike that region, the plants here are not thorny at all, but rather lush and green. Every time I crossed the landscape, I'd think to myself: 'Imagine how beautiful it must be here in summer!', but then I remembered that it actually was summer.

Despite this seeming inhospitality, this area was inhabited as early as pre-historic times, of which many ruins are still around in the form of dolmen and Stone Forts.

The most famous dolmen is that of Pulnabrone, which is located just north of the route. The famous Cahercowell Fort is situated on the route itself, and to get there you will first need to cross a deep valley. After you have passed Cavan, the route will first ascend to the highland, but then you will get to a deep valley that you will need to follow straight down before going up again. It's only a short stretch, but it's pretty intense, and I had to actually walk the last part coming from the other side. These types of sneaky little hills are inevitable on any route. After all, if you want to explore the magically car-free Burren you'll need to make a few concessions along the way. The other hills up to Lisdoonvarna are more bicycle-friendly.

From Lisdoonvarna the route follows the N67 to Ennistymon. As an alternative, you might consider completing this part of the journey by using some of the smaller roads, as I suggested. The only drawback of this alternative is a very small barking dog that tried to bite me. While the N67 is not one of the busiest roads, this may still be an appealing idea. The road meanders up and down the landscape, which is not nearly as rugged as in The Burren.

Ennistymon is a small town where you'll find all the facilities you need. A particularly beautiful sight is the waterfall and the view over the river across the bridge. From the main street you head into a small street to the right, after which you'll arrive at this picture-perfect spot.

If you're looking for more sophisticated entertainment, head for Lahinch on the coast. There you'll find – along with surfers in the bay and several golf courses – amenities such as hotels, clubs and restaurants. You will need to stock up on food before leaving Ennistymon, as there won't be any more shops for the next 35 kilometres.

After following the wide valley, the route will gradually take you up to the valley edge. As you won't actually be able to make it very far, it's not really much of a climb. The landscape here is a combination of farmland and forest. You'll have to climb up the occasional hill and head down again. The hamlets here have names, but other than a few closed pubs all you'll find are houses and farms. There is also a sizeable fox population in this area, and sometimes one is caught off guard by a passing cyclist or car. There is more woodland on top of the hill, and there are large windmills at the highest point of the hill to catch the wind – it's a good alternative to peat.

Dogs are very common in Ireland. Many are used as guard dogs, watching over enclosed areas, and some of them are chained. Others don't need a chain, but are alert and a little curious to see if someone will show up and liven up their boring day. One particular dog that I found dozing in front of a house saw me cycling and decided to join me. Tail wagging, he followed me as I slowly cycled up the hill. I enjoyed his company, and started talking to him as he continued happily trailing along. After three kilometres, the dog was still there and I started to get worried. I raised my voice and sternly told him to go home, but he just looked at me with his head cocked. After continuing for another kilometre, I suddenly had visions of completing the remainder of my trip with a dog in tow. After another kilometre the road wound downhill and I started pedalling very fast. It was a bit too fast for the dog, and I didn't call him back after that.

The town of Kilmihil has a shop and a pub, which is all you really need in this area. You're getting close to the river Shannon now. The slopes are getting deeper and after 10 kilometres you'll spot the river. On the other side, you see the tall pipe of the power plant in Tarbert guiding you like a beacon. The ferry usually sails every 30 minutes, and the journey across costs around 5 euro (2011 price).

Accommodation

Map 24

Inveran
  B&B Tigh Chualain, Kilroe East, ph: (0)91 553609

Spiddal
  Hotel An Cruiscin Lán, (0)91 553148
  Teach Osta Na Pairce Hotel, ph: (0)91 553159
  There are more than 5 B&Bs in Spiddal

Barna
  Hotel The Twelve, ph: (0)91 597000
  B&B Abbeyville, ph: (0)91 592430

Map 25

Galway City
  There are more than 5 hotels and B&Bs in Galway.

More information at the TIC (Tourist Information Centre).
  Salthill Caravan & Camping, Knocknacarna, Salthill, ph: (0)91 523972
  Ballyloughane Caravan & Camping Park, Ballyloughane Beach, Renmore, ph: (0)91 752029

Map 26

Oranmore
  Coach House Hotel, ph: (0)91 788367
  Maldron Hotel Galway, ph: (0)91 792244
  Oranmore Lodge Hotel, ph: (0)91 794400
  Ramada Encore, ph: (0)91 383300
  There are more than 5 B&Bs in Oranmore

Map 27

Kilcolgan
  B&B Hollyoak, Kinvara Road, Ballinderreen, ph: (0)91 637165

Kinvara
  Merriman Hotel, Main Street, ph: (0)91 638222
  Doorus House Youth Hostel, ph: (0)91 637512
  There are more than 5 B&Bs in Kinvarra

Map 28

Carran
  Hostel Clares Rock, ph: (0)65 708 9129
  B&B Deelin House, ph: (0)65 708 9105

Lisdoonvarna
  There are more than 5 hotels and B&Bs in Lisdoonvarna. For more information, please contact TIC.
  Hostel The Sleepzone, ph: (0)65 707 4036

Map 29

Doolin

Hotel Doolin, ph: (0)65 707 4111

Hotel Tin Gan Ean House, ph: (0)65 707 5726

Aille River Hostel, ph: (0)65 707 4260

Fisherstreet House Hostel, ph: (0)65 707 4421

Flanagans Village Hostel, ph: (0)65 707 4564

Paddys Doolin Hostel, Sea Road, ph: (0)65 707 4421

Rainbow Hostel, ph: (0)65 707 4415

Aran View House Hotel, ph: (0)65 707 4061

Ballinalacken Castle, Coast Road, ph: (0)65 707 4025

There are more than 5 B&Bs in Doolin. For more information, please contact the TIC of Lisdoonvarna.

Doolin Riverside Caravan & Camping Park, ph: (0)65 707 4498

Nagles Doolin Caravan & Camping Park, ph: (0)65 707 4458

Liscannor

Cliffs Of Moher Hotel, Main Street, ph: (0)65 708 6770

Logues Liscannor Hotel, ph: (0)65 708 6000

B&B Castleview Farmhouse, Cliffs of Mother Rd, Clahan, ph: (0)65 708 1590

B&B Harbour Sunset Farmhouse, Rannagh, ph: (0)65 708 1039

B&B Mother Lodge, Cliffs of Mother, ph: (0)65 708 1269

B&B Sea Haven, ph: (0)65 708 1385

Map 30

Ennistymon

Falls Hotel, ph: (0)65 707 1004

B&B Grovemount House, Lahinch Road, ph: (0)65 707 1431 (well-groomed)

B&B Hillbrook Farm, Lahinch Road, ph: (0)65 708 1039

B&B Pairc An Fhia, Deerpark Upper, ph: (0)65 707 1134

B&B Station House, Ennis Road, ph: (0)65 707 1149

B&B Sunset, Kilcornan, ph: (0)65 707 1527

Lahinch

Lahinch Golf And Leisure Hotel, ph: (0)65 708 1100

Sancta Maria Hotel, ph: (0)65 7081041

The Atlantic Hotel, Main Street, ph: (0)65 708 1049

Lahinch Hostel, Church Street, ph: (0)65 708 1040

The Shamrock Inn, Main Street, ph: (0)65 708 1700

Vaughan Lodge, Ennistymon Road, ph: (0)65 708 1111

There are more than 5 B&Bs in Lahinch. For more information, contact the TIC.

Lahinch Camping and Caravan Park, ph: (0)65 81424

CYCLE SHOPS/REPAIRS:

Galway

Kearney Cycles (hire), Terryland Retail Park, Headford Rd, ph: (0)91 563356

West Side Cycles, Unit 1, West Side Business Centre, ph: (0)91 525007

Europa Bicycles, Hunter Building, Earls Island, ph: (0)91 563355

Walsh Richard Cycles, 11 Headford rd, Woodquay, ph: (0)91 565710

Ennis

Tierneys Cycles (Clare Bike Hire), 17 Abbey Street, ph: (0)65 682 9433

Harry's Cycles Centre, Gort Road Business Park, ph: (0)65 684 2300

Small ferry to Doolin.

28

1. At descent keep right on road, afterwards keep to the left.
2. At T-junction with right of way road ⬅↑ upwards. 1st road ⬆➡ upwards.
3. Deep valley, walking allowed.
4. Crossing with right of way road ↑.
5. At T-junction ⬆➡ and then 650m at T-junction sharp ⬅↑.
6. 1st road ⬆➡ and after sharp bend to the right 1st road ⬅↑.
7. At T-Junction ⬅↑ and 1st road ⬆➡.

Carran — Caherconell — Lisdoonvarna
0 — 5,5 — 17

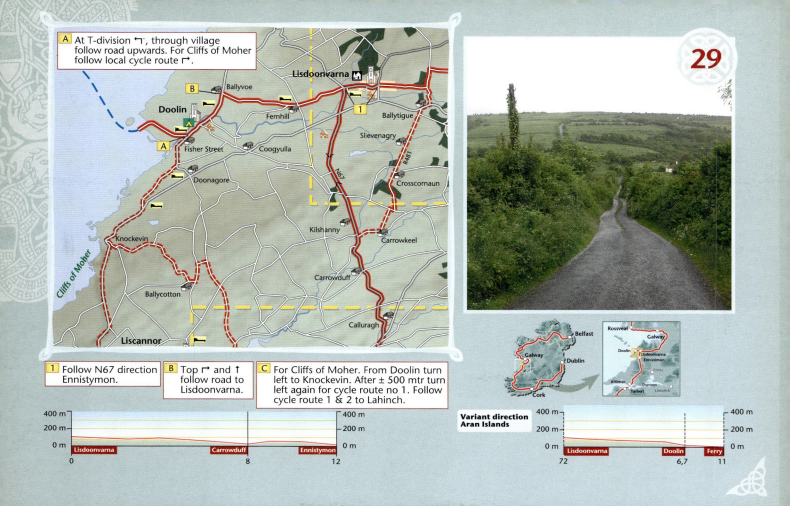

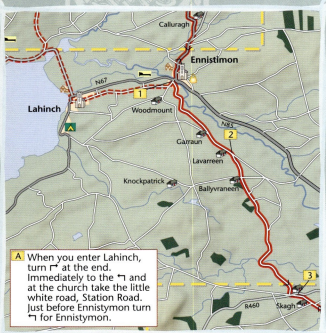
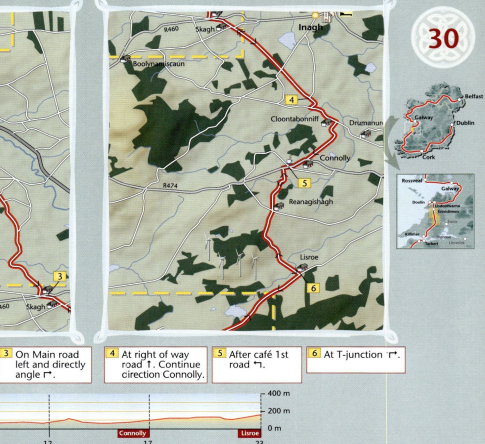

A When you enter Lahinch, turn → at the end. Immediately to the ← and at the church take the little white road, Station Road. Just before Ennistymon turn ← for Ennistymon.

1 In Ennistymon, over the bridge ← and ← again.

2 Continue following road and at V-division angle ↗. Follow direction Connolly.

3 On Main road left and directly angle →.

4 At right of way road ↑. Continue direction Connolly.

5 After café 1st road ←.

6 At T-junction →.

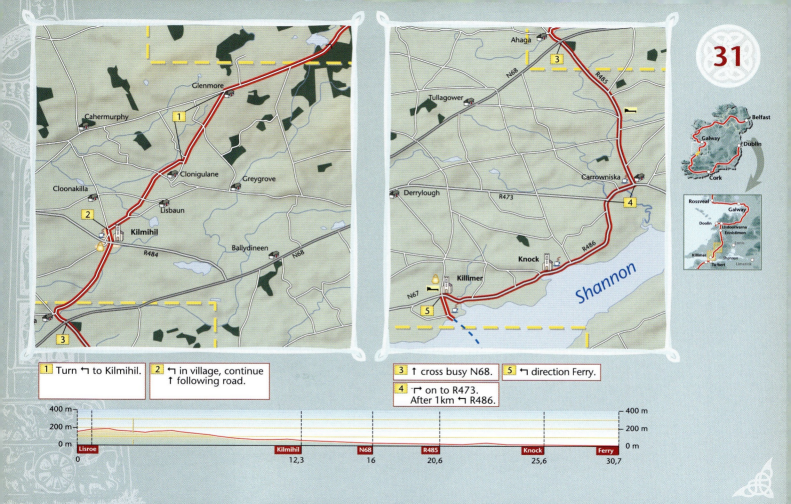

Kerry and Dingle

From the ferry to Tralee, the land is almost completely flat, making for a nice change. Just before Ballylongford you will pass the ruins of the 15th-century Franciscan monastery of Lislaughtin. It currently serves as a cemetery, which means you need to walk along the edges of the graves to get a proper look. There is something mystical about this place, and in 1998, at sundown, someone saw the ghost of a woman rising up from the mist.

Located north-west of Ballylongford are the ruins of Carrigafoyle Castle, but it's not really exceptional enough (and located too far off the road) for a visit. After Ballylongford, the route leads across a hill and from there on to Lisselton. Slightly further to the west lies the town of Ballybunion, a resort that offers a number of amenities. After Lisselton, the landscape is flat – when I crossed the river I was reminded of parts of the eastern Netherlands. Right after the bridge (if you've turned left), you'll pass a halting site for Irish Travellers. In the past, the Travelling Community made a living by performing odd jobs for people; now they fix and sell second-hand cars and train greyhounds and horses. There are approximately 22,000 Travellers in Ireland today, the majority of whom live near the cities. Only 1,400 live in rural communities. Although the birth rate in the Traveller community is significantly higher than in the general population, the death rate among children is also ten times higher, as are the number of traffic fatalities. The average age in the Traveller population is thirty-nine.

As you continue on this road, you will pass Rattoo Round Tower, which was built in the tenth century. These towers are believed to have been built primarily as bell towers for the surrounding community. Since the door to the entrance is located several metres aboveground, it was once believed that these towers were used as watchtowers to look out for Vikings and as a place where monks could retreat in the event of an attack. Since a simple fire at the bottom of the tower was enough to smoke out the monks, it is now believed that the elevated door had more to do with ensuring a solid construction, as many towers were built with a limited foundation and a low entrance would weaken the construction.

Further down, we head left to Tralee, taking us past the ruins of Ardfert Cathedral. This impressive cathedral was built in the 12th century, in the location where a monastery was established by St. Brendan in the 6th century.

The Cathedral was destroyed in 1641 during the Irish Uprising. There is an admission charge to view the cathedral.

To ensure that you will cross quiet roads to get to Tralee, the route runs across a low hill, from where you'll have a beautiful view of the Dingle Peninsula and the Bay of Tralee.

Tralee is a lively regional centre that has all the facilities you'll need. The town is famous for the annual International Rose of Tralee festival, where the most beautiful girl of Irish origin is crowned with the title of 'Rose of Tralee'. Candidates from all over Ireland, as well as from Irish communities in other parts of the world, are selected in qualifying rounds. The girls must not only be beautiful, but also possess the virtues celebrated in the ancient, eponymous ballad 'The Rose of Tralee'. The festival is held each year at the end of August, and it's hard to find accommodation in the town during that time.

But even without any Irish beauties on display, Tralee is well worth a visit. The Kerry County Museum lets you discover the history of Southern Ireland. In addition to excellent exhibition rooms, the museum also has an audiovisual department where you'll be taken right back to medieval times.

Tralee is also the best place to stay if you're visiting Dingle, a peninsula that is one of the highlights of Southern Ireland. The place is not yet over-run by tourists making their way across the Kerry Peninsula.

The north coast of Dingle features beautiful, white, sandy beaches against a backdrop of tall mountaintops. Castlegregory is another lovely place to visit, especially the pub, which has a charming courtyard where you can enjoy the sunshine, a good meal and a pint of Guinness even on blustery days. From the north side, the Connor Pass leads to Dingle Town. At 456 metres, this is the highest spot in southern Ireland, and as you might expect it offers some of the most stunning panoramas. The north side of the pass is small, but impressive, and going uphill here is quite a challenge. I toured the pass from the south and I think I stopped just as many times to take photographs as I would have done otherwise to catch my breath. Still, the view changes at each turn and stopping to take that one special photograph is part of what makes this journey so much fun. The great thing about cycling is that you can stop in areas that are inaccessible to motorists – just that part of the turn that you know will make for a beautiful picture.

I found Dingle Town itself to be a bit of a letdown. I may have gone there a decade too late, as the local restaurant business seemed to cater completely for mass tourism, offering everything from Indian Tandoori places to the westernmost hotdog joint in Europe.

Slea Head Drive runs west of Dingle. This road passes along one of the most beautiful parts of Dingle, one that is rich in historical ruins dating back to the time of ancient monks. Slea Head Drive is indicated clockwise for motorists, which is a good reason for us to follow the route the other way around. It first takes us to the Gallarus Oratory, a small, early Christian church dating back 1,200 years that's shaped like an upturned boat. Near Dunquin, you can see the Great Blasket Island, which, despite its isolation – or maybe because of it – produced three major Irish writers. The island has been uninhabited since 1953. Close to Slea Head you will find the Beehives – these were small, stone monk cells where the monks retreated in order to fast. The full tour is only 63 kilometres, but there is so much to see on the way that a visit could easily take an entire day.

From Tralee to the heart of Kerry, near Macgillycuddy's Reeks, the shortest road right after Tralee runs across a relatively low pass, but it does have a firm short climb, a calf-biter to give it a name. You could cycle around it, of course, but that would take eight kilometres, which is not really worth it. The descent feels good – like a long straight line downward. The scenery is pleasant here: a combination of pastures and forest. There are also a number of horse-breeding farms around the area.

As you approach Killarney, the landscape becomes more park-like. The route does not pass through Killarney itself, as the town has become very touristy.

You should first head towards the mountains, which is where you'll find the highest point in Ireland, just over 1,000 metres. The Gap of Dunloe is a famous pass that runs through these mountains. Hikers, cyclists and horse-drawn carriages all follow this path up the hill. The carriages are parked outside Kate Kearney's Cottage, offering rides to tourists. The hill is fairly steep, the road is a bit uneven, and because of the large number of tourists I considered not including this pass in our route. Still, a hot cup of coffee at Kate Kearney's Coffeepot tastes delicious, and the view in the distance will make you glad you stopped at this pass road.

The route now runs around the mountains, to the beautiful and tranquil Ballybeama Pass. The mountaintops are often shrouded in mist, and about halfway through you pass a wildly-flowing river. The road is smooth, descends gradually, and the views are spectacular. You pass mountain lake through a low pass. Both at this lake and before, while heading down the road, I saw signs indicating unofficial campsites.

Once you've passed this lake, you will end up in the hamlet of Glencar; there is a pub where you can get a drink and a sandwich, which is just the ticket for the next stretch of the journey.

The route now leads you around the mountain, on the way to the actual pass. The scenery is gorgeous here. During my trip, sunny spells were followed by showers, and as I got closer to the pass the rain started to pour down harder and the water came seeping out of every crack in the rocks, flowing, rushing and splashing. The road first ascends gradually until the last few kilometres, which requires pedalling hard through a narrow pass. With *Lord of the Rings* in mind, this area is what I imagine Mordor must look like. On top of the pass I was almost blown over by a strong wind, forcing me to stop completely for brief periods. There was something almost ghostlike about the place, as if hidden forces were trying to keep me there. Still, it was a wonderful experience: although the pass is not very high, the views are something right out of a old picture book.

I did not feel unlucky because of the rain; it actually seemed to me to be part of the scenery, although I'm sure it would be just as beautiful without the rain. The descent starts out just as precipitous as the last climb, after which it gradually becomes less steep. As you head down to the sea,

the barren land makes way for woodland. For the last few kilometres to Kenmare, the route runs through a slightly busier road. Kenmare is a pleasant town with shops and a couple of lively pubs. After Kenmare you cross the bridge, where the main route bends left to Glengariff. If you're interested in a slightly longer tour through Beara, you should turn right here. The scenery in Beara is just as beautiful as that of the trail around Kerry, but it is much more open and the panoramas are wider. The most beautiful views can be found on top of Healy Pass, which is very accessible, and, as with the previous pass, only the last two kilometres are challenging. I was unlucky in that I had planned to climb this pass from the south on a stormy day. After being literally blown off my bike twice during the last two kilometres, I finally gave up. A cycling mate has assured me that his experience a few years before was fantastic, so I would not want to keep anyone from following this route. I just hope that it won't rain on my next visit to this area.

The main route first runs parallel to the main road or through the valley. If there are no other options, the route joins the main road, which is fortunately fairly wide, and the traffic wasn't too bad either. The ascent is gradual at first, only to become steeper as you head up to the highest point, after passing through a short tunnel. Here, you head into a small tunnel less than two hundred metres long, so it's not really a scary experience despite the darkness. On the other side you head down into the Bantry Bay, where the views are beautiful.

I was just unlucky the day I was there as it was foggy. I am determined to revisit the area sometime in the future. The descent is fast and very satisfying, and down below is the town of Glengariff, the centre of the subtropical part of Ireland.

Traditionally a favourite resort of well-heeled English tourists, Glengariff is surrounded by mountains on all sides, and at the end of one of the estuaries

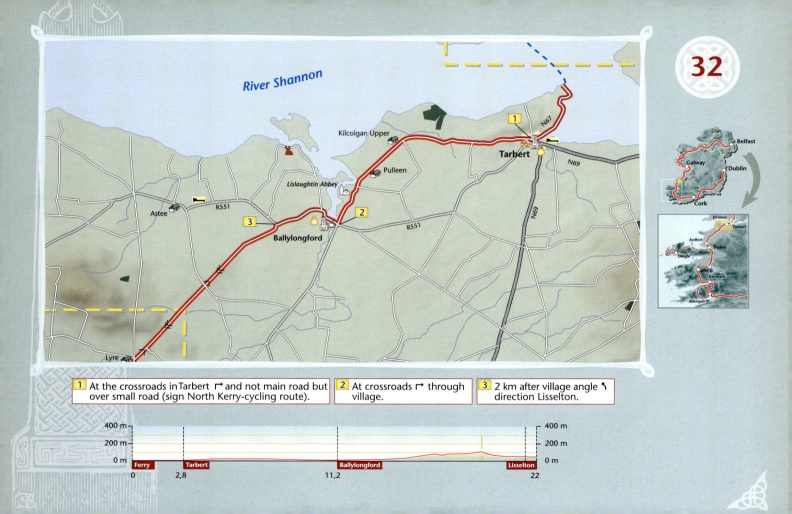

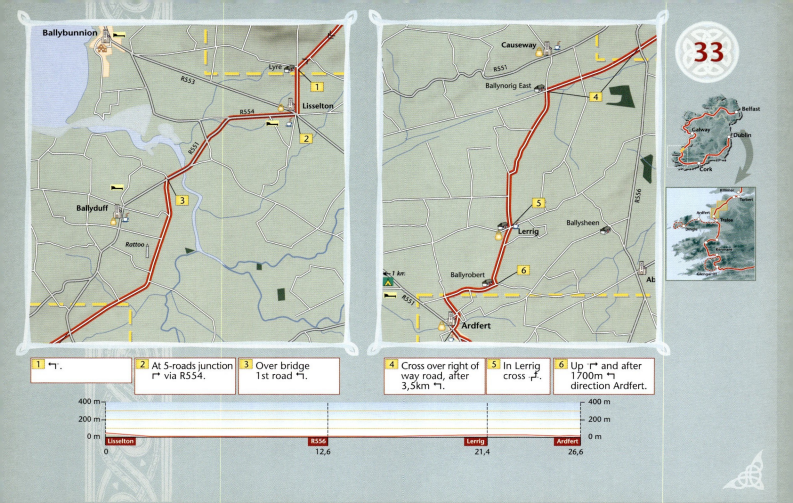

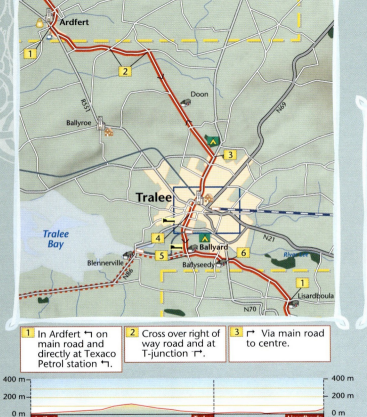

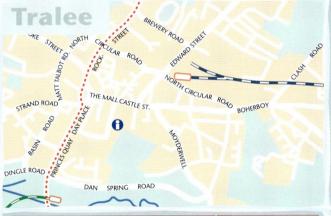

34

1 In Ardfert ↰ on main road and directly at Texaco Petrol station ↰.	**2** Cross over right of way road and at T-junction ↱.	**3** ↱ Via main road to centre.
4 Leave Tralee via Princes Quay, at roundabout ↑.	**5** At crossing ↰.	**7** ↑ Upwards with the road, slightly left and continue following road.
	6 At crossing with main road ↑.	

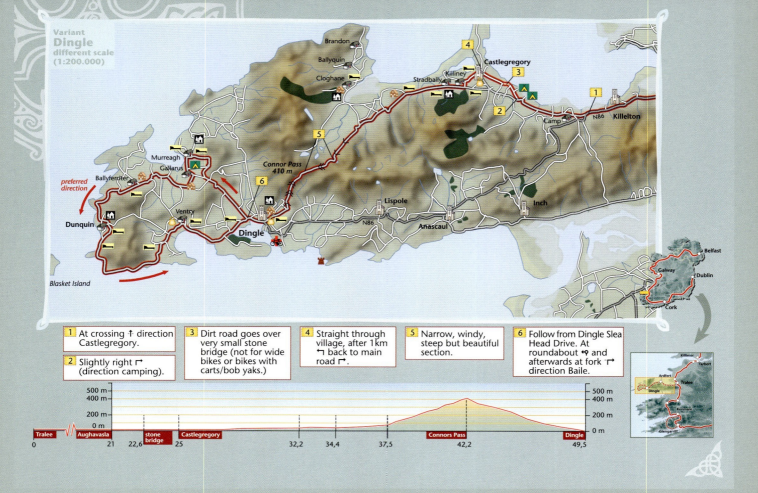

Dingle North beach

Connor's Pass

Beer garden Castlegregory

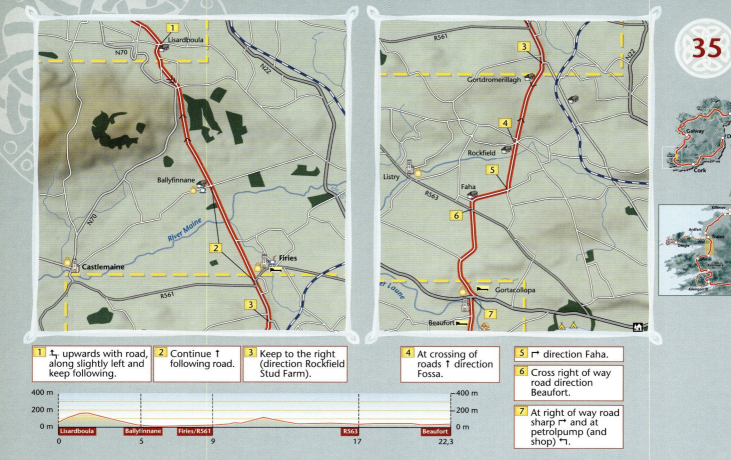

MacGillycuddy's Reeks   **Into Mordor**
On the way to Ballybeama pass

| 1 | ↑ direction Gap of Dunloe. | 2 | ↱ direction Glencar. | 3 | Follow road keeping left. | 4 | Keeping left. | 5 | At T-junction ↰. |

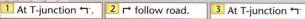
1 At T-junction ↰. 2 ↱ follow road. 3 At T-junction ↰

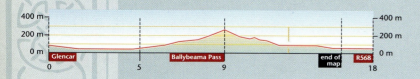

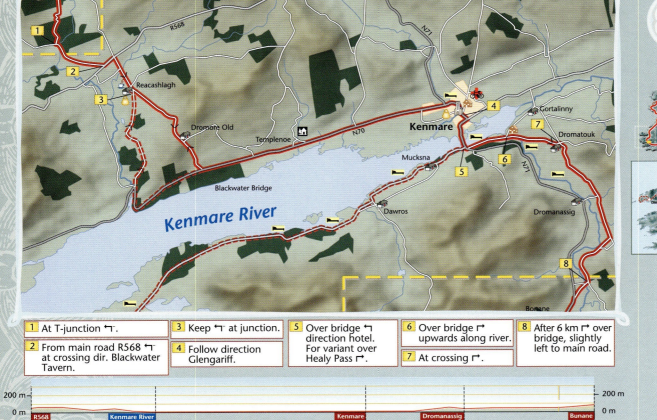

1. At T-junction ←.
2. From main road R568 ← at crossing dir. Blackwater Tavern.
3. Keep ← at junction.
4. Follow direction Glengariff.
5. Over bridge ← direction hotel. For variant over Healy Pass →.
6. Over bridge → upwards along river.
7. At crossing →.
8. After 6 km → over bridge, slightly left to main road.

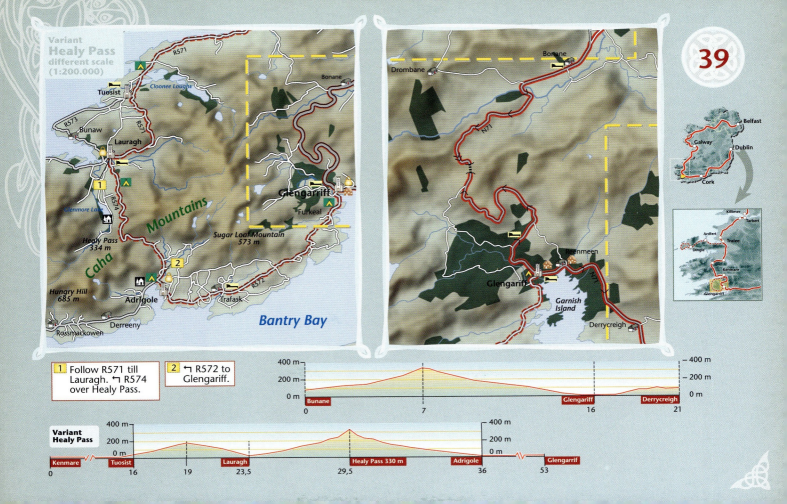

GLENGARIFF

INCHCULLAN

GARINISH ISLAND

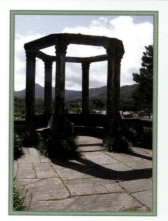

the weather does indeed feel very balmy. The vegetation here is lush. On the coast you'll find Garinish Island, with its beautifully landscaped, Italian-style gardens. The boat tour (sans bike) passes a seal colony. The tour is not cheap (around € 10 per person), and on the island you will need to pay again to gain access.

Accommodation

Map 32

Tarbert

    Kirby's Lanterns Hotel, Glin/Tarbert Coast Road, ph: (0)68 36210

    Hostel The Ferry House, The Square, ph: (0)68 36555

    B&B Dillane's Farmhouse, Listowel Road, ph: (0)68 36242

    B&B Keldun House, Main Street, ph: (0)68 36405

    B&B Knight's Haven, Tarbert/Glin Road, ph: (0)68 34541

Ballylongford

    B&B Castle View House, Carrig Island, ph: (0)68 43304

Map 33

Ballyduff

    B&B Hill View, Leigh, ph: (0)66 7131806

Map 34

Ardfert

    Banna Beach Hotel, ph: (0)66 713 4103

    Camping Sir Rogers C & C Park, Banna, ph: (0)66 713 4730

Tralee

    There are more than five hotels and B&Bs in Tralee. For more information contact TIC.

    Hostel Castle Hotel, Castle Street, ph: (0)66 712 5167

    Finnegans Hostel, 17 Denny Street, ph: (0)66 712 7610

    Camping Woodlands Park, Dan Spring Road, ph: (0)66 712 1235

Map Dingle

    Dingle Bay Hotel, Strand Street, ph: (0)66 914 1231

    Dingle Benners Hotel, Main Street, ph: (0)66 915 1638

    Dingle Skelling Hotel, ph: (0)66 9150200

    Hostel Dingle Harbour Lodge, The Wood, ph: (0)66 915 1577

    There are more than five B&Bs in Dingle. For more information contact TIC.

    Camping Pratory House Camping, Gallarus, ph: (0)66 915 5143

Castlegregory

    Crutch's Hillville House Hotel, Fermoyle Beach, ph: (0)66 713 8118

    There are more than five B&Bs in and around Castlegregory.

    Camping Anchor Caravan Park, ph: (0)66 713 9157

    Green Acres Caravan Park, Aughacasla, ph: (0)66 713 9158

Map 36

Beaufort

    B&B Beaufort Lodge, Coolmagort, ph: (0)64 24822

    B&B Hollybough House, Cappagh, ph: (0)64 6644255

    B&B Mountain View, Gap of Dunloe, ph: (0)64 442121

    Fossa Caravan & Camping Park, ph: (0)64 314 97 (open 21/03 – 30/09)

    Beech Grove Caravan & Camping Park, ph: (0)64 317 27 (open 15/03 – 4/10)

Map 38
Kenmare

There are more than five hotels and B&Bs in Kenmare.
For more information contact TIC.
Failte Hostel, Shelbourne Street, ph: (0)64 42333
Greenwood Hostel, Greenane, Killarney, ph: (0)64 668 9247
Kenmare Lodge Hostel, 27 Main Street, ph: (0)64 40662

Map 39
Glengarriff

Caseys Hotel, ph: (0)27 276 3010
Eccles Hotel, ph: (0)27 63003
Glengarriff Park Hotel, Main Street, ph: (0)27 63000
Murphys Village Hostel, ph: (0)27 63555
There are in Glengarriff more than five B&Bs. Contact TIC.

Via the Healy Pass

Glanmore Lake Youth Hostel, ph: (0)64 83181
Camping The Peacock, Coornagillagh, Tuosist, ph: (0)64 84287
(Dutch owners, also trekker huts)
Creveen Lodge Caravan Park, Lauragh, ph: (0)64 83131
Hostel & Camping Hungry Hill Lodge, Adrigole Harbour, ph: (0)27 60228

Map 40
Ballylickey

Seaview Hotel, ph: (0)27 50073
Eagle Point Camping, ph: (0)27 50630

CYCLE SHOPS/REPAIRS:
Tralee

O'Halloran Cycles, 83 Boherbue, ph: (0)66 712 2820
Caball Jim Himself, Staughtons Row, ph: (0)66 712 1654
Halfords, Manor West Retail, ph: (0)66 710 3730

Dingle

Paddys Bicycles Hire, Dykegate St, ph: (0)66 915 2311

Killarney

David O'Sullivan, Lower New St & Beech Rd, ph: (0)64 663 1282
The Big Little Bike Shop, Woodlawn Rd, ph: (0)64 34294

Kenmare

Kenmare Cycle Centre, 37/38 Henry Street

Bantry, 10 km south of Ballylickey:

Nigel's Bicycle Shop, Newtown, ph: (0)27 52657

Cork
and the South East

As the name indicates, the Cork to Beara Cycleway is a cycling route that runs from Cork to the Beara Peninsula, and I thought it would be a good idea to incorporate this trail into our route. Well, the trail was not so easy to follow. Not only were several signs damaged, another sign pointed in the wrong direction, leading me to take the wrong turn and continue for a couple of kilometres. I later wished I had actually stayed on the 'wrong' road, as once I was back on the official trail more misery awaited me: the quality of the road gradually deteriorated, and one steep hill followed another. The highest point was so steep that I couldn't even push my bike anymore and actually had to pull it behind me. The most precipitous hill had a steepness of approximately 18%, but cycling down took me just as long. Due to the poor road surface, the potholes and bends in the road and the stray bits of gravel, I was forced to press down hard on the brakes and walk down the hill for my descent. I was absolutely livid. To add insult to injury, the scenery wasn't anything special either, and after I had finally stopped for a hot drink in the nearest village, the route continued across several main roads, after which the traffic only became worse. At that point, I still had 30 kilometres to go. Some cycling route …! The next day I returned by bus and then continued cycling again, now on my own route.

It sometimes seems as if local cycling routes in Ireland are all planned by Olympic-level mountain bikers, all under the age of thirty and travelling without any baggage!

The route now runs through the regional road across the Cousane Pass. Fortunately, this road is very manageable – nice and smooth and not too steep. There's not too much traffic around either.

The descent is easy, and after that the road meanders through a wide valley. Only after Coppeen is it worth the effort of looking for small roads again, as most of these roads before Coppeen lead to ascents that are somewhat tedious.

From Crookstown, the route is almost completely flat, until you get to the outskirts of Cork, where it starts to get hilly again.

On the way you will pass the ruins of the ancient Kilcrea Friary. This site is located somewhat off the beaten path, however, if you did not visit the site at Ardfert, go take a look here, it is free. The next town over, Killumney, has some excellent pubs. Once you pass this point, you will soon enter the sprawling suburbs of Cork.

This second-largest city in Ireland (with a population of 186,000), Cork is a bustling town renowned for its nightlife. The residents feel their city is the country's real capital, as they were traditionally more resistant to British rule than were the Dubliners. This is why Cork was traditionally nicknamed 'the Rebel County'. They have a point, as it is true that Dublin was under the influence of the British for a longer period of time. Cork was founded at the mouth of the River Lee, near a swamp, which is indeed the literal meaning of the name 'Corcaigh', Cork's Irish name.

After St Finbar established a convent school here in the sixth century, a settlement evolved which was to eventually become a city. After Vikings had initially invaded the town to raid it, they later ended up settling here with the purpose of establishing a trading post. The Vikings started becoming involved in local life, which was to happen again later when the Normans settled here.

However, rebellion against the English has always been strong in Cork, as witnessed by the fact that part of the city was destroyed on several occasions.

Cork has always been a centre of productivity, with the butter trade being just one of the industries that flourished here, with exports to Europe and North America. Even today, Cork is still known as Ireland's most productive city.

The city is attractive; the centre is situated between two arms of the River Lee and is made up of broader main streets, such as the Grand Parade, along with many attractive little side streets lined with cafés and restaurants. The Shandon Church dominates the north bank of the river, while the south bank is home to the beautiful St Finbarre's Cathedral. It's worth stopping at the English Market, an indoor market that sells a wide range of food items.

The route departs the city through the Marina. At the end of the Marina you'll find the beautiful Blackrock Castle, but before you get there, the route will lead you to a cycling path over an old railway track to the right. This is a perfect cycling track leading all the way out of town. You can take the ferry to cross the estuary between Lough Mahon and Cobh Harbour ('Cobh' is pronounced 'Cove'). This was the place from where many thousands of Irish men, women and children boarded ships to America during and after the Famine. Many of them did not survive the journey.

Cobh was also the last stop for the Titanic in 1912, and three years later the Lusitania was torpedoed by a German submarine.

These days, it's a perfectly peaceful little town. The Queenstown Story (Cobh was previously called 'Queenstown'), a museum located in a former railway depot, is devoted to Cobh's history, including its maritime history.

The route continues across a small dyke leading you back to the land.

Midleton is a small town that used to be home to the Jameson Distillery. The old buildings and installations have been fully updated, and you can take a tour of the building to learn about traditional whiskey-making. If you fancy a glass right after the tour, they sell the stuff on the premises as well.

Located just south of Midleton is the town of Cloyne, which has a pretty church and a Round Tower. However, our route runs east through the flat, fertile coastal area, only to reach the sea at Youghal. There is also an old railway line that runs from Midleton to Youghal, which could actually be converted into a cycle track.

Youghal (pronounced 'Yawl') is a pretty little harbour town at the mouth of the Blackwater River. It features a special lighthouse, and a clock gate that the main street runs through.

The area near the Blackwater River is beautiful and park-like. You first cycle along the water before heading into the dense woods. When you get out of the woods you'll see grass fields, surrounded by trees. The way the landscape here is organised and the way the town of Lismore is maintained seems almost Swiss in its neatness, showing a real love for and pride in the local environment. Lismore has a beautiful castle that used to serve as the Bishop's seat – the garden is open to the public, but the building isn't. The small town is also home to the beautiful St Carthage's Cathedral and a Heritage Centre. Cappoquin is also located in a very scenic spot around the Blackwater River, which is known for its good fishing (lots of salmon and trout).

Behind Cappoquin you'll see the hills of the Knockmealdown Mountains. Note that the name of these mountains is not actually 'knock me down' –

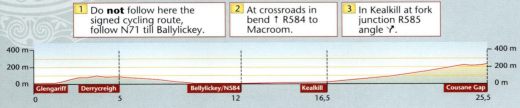

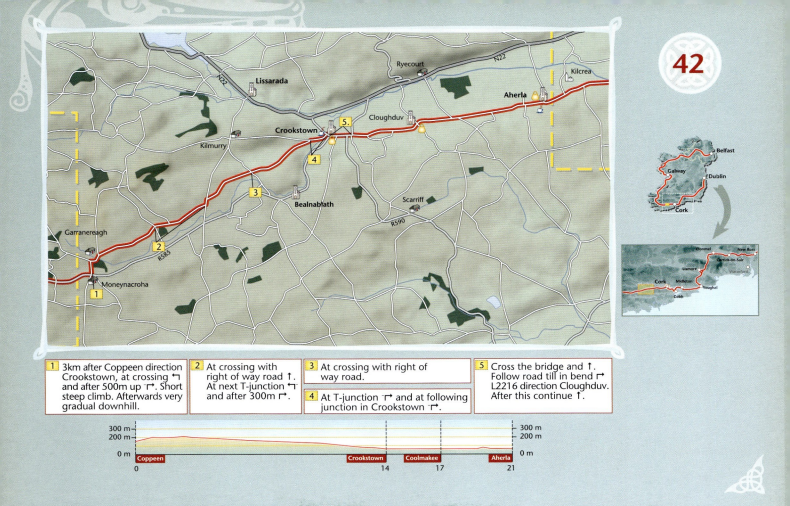

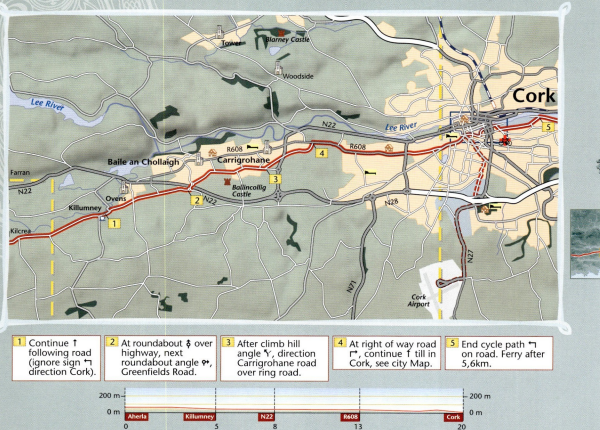

43

1. Continue ↑ following road (ignore sign ↰ direction Cork).
2. At roundabout ⊗ over highway, next roundabout angle ⤻, Greenfields Road.
3. After climb hill angle Y, direction Carrigrohane road over ring road.
4. At right of way road ↱, continue ↑ till in Cork, see city Map.
5. End cycle path ↰ on road. Ferry after 5,6km.

Aherla	Killumney	N22	R608	Cork
0	5	8	13	20

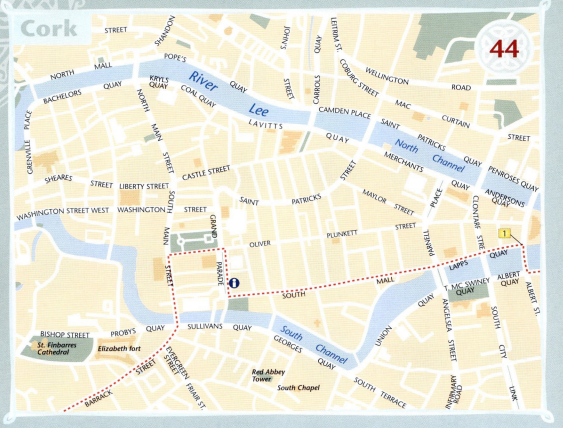

Cork

44

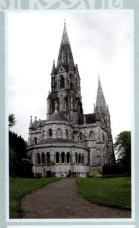

Saint Finbarre's Cathedral

1 Over bridge ⤴ with the road right and at roundabout ↩ (Becomes Centre Park Road).

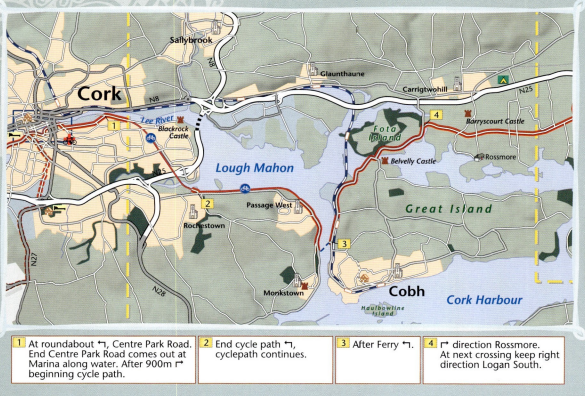

| **1** | At roundabout ↰, Centre Park Road. End Centre Park Road comes out at Marina along water. After 900m ↱ beginning cycle path. | **2** | End cycle path ↰, cyclepath continues. | **3** | After Ferry ↰. | **4** | ↱ direction Rossmore. At next crossing keep right direction Logan South. |

Cobh

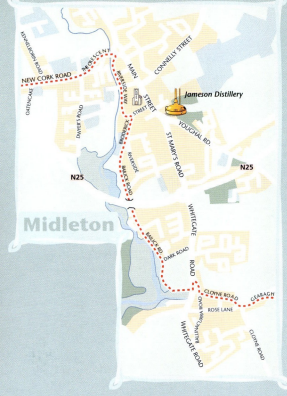

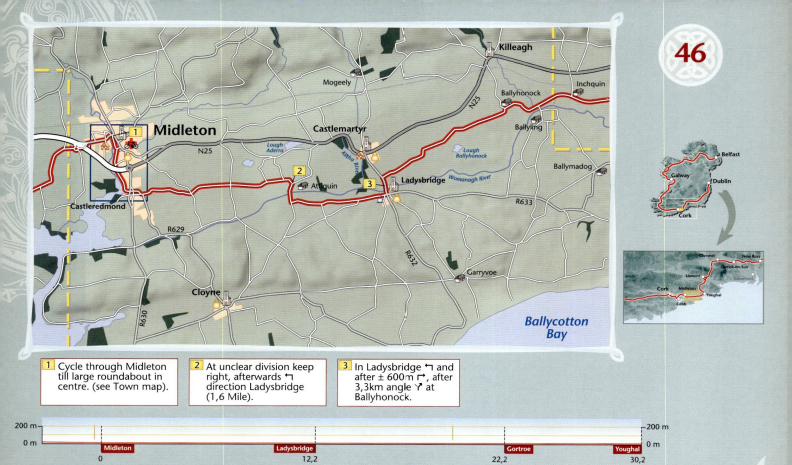

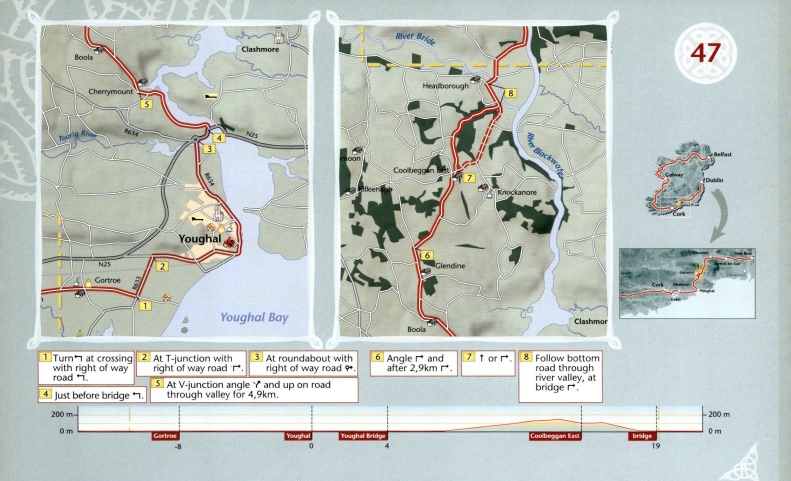

Lismore & The Knockmealdown Mountains

49

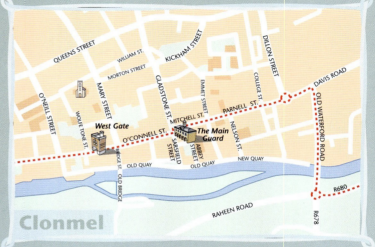

| 1 | In Newcastle ↑. | 2 | Angle ↱. | 3 | ↱ main road R665 follow till in Clonmel, or ↰ and then ↱, steep climb, but calm till Clonmel. |

CLONMEL

RIVER SUIR

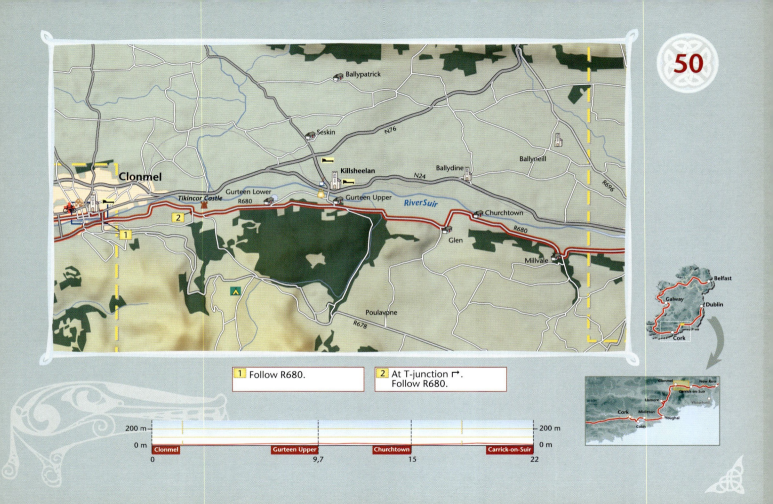

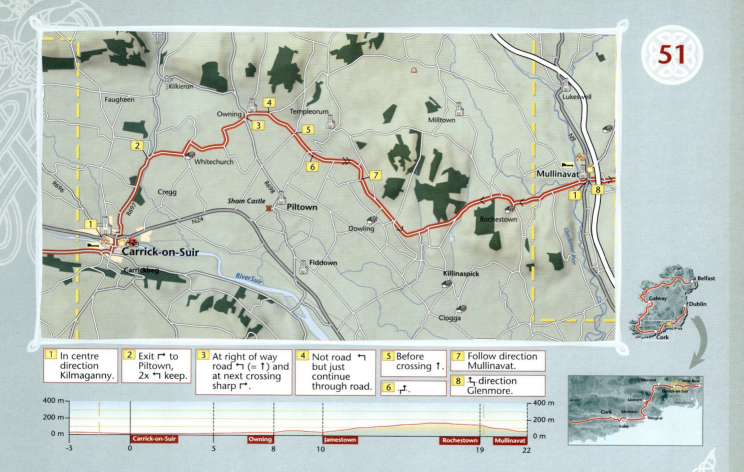

climbing this side takes a bit of effort but is never really heavy. The panoramas gradually become wider and more beautiful here. Mount Mellleray Convent, which is situated on the parallel hill flank, was built by Cistercian monks who settled here after the Reformation.

From the top you can get a good view of the other hilltops.

The descent here is a little steeper than the climb. On the other side, you end up in the valley of the River Suir. This river, too, is known for its abundant fish, although it's a bit narrower than the Blackwater River.

Situated at the foot of the Comeragh Mountains, Clonmel is one of the liveliest towns in the southern part of Tipperary. Like in Youghal, you enter the city through a gate. On the other side of the main street you'll find the Guard House.

Between Clonmel and Carrick-on-Suir, the route follows the River Suir. Just outside Clonmel, on your left-hand side, you'll see a beautiful old bridge across the river. The route follows the south bank, and occasionally you will cycle around the hillside before making your way down again.

While significantly smaller than Clonmel, Carrick is home to the ruins of Ormond Castle, an old Elizabethan manor, as well as being the birthplace of Irish cycling legend Sean Kelly. The route then continues through a stretch of prosperous farmland, around Waterford and up to New Ross. Due to the many highs and lows here, you will often need to ascend or descend.

New Ross is where you'll find the first link across the Barrow. The town is located on the east side of the river. The sights on the quay include a replica of the Dunbrody Famine Ship, on which many thousands of Irish people set sail for 'America' in 1870. Many among them did not survive the forty-five-day passage. The centre of New Ross, with its narrow streets, is small, but it is the last of the larger towns on our route before we continue our journey towards the Wicklow Mountains.

ACCOMMODATION

Map 44
Cork
   In Cork are more than five hotels, hostels and B&Bs. For more information contact TIC.

Map 45
Cobh
   Bella Vista Hotel, Bishop's Road, ph: (0)21 481 2450
   Commodore Hotel, ph: (0)21 481 1277
   Watersedge Hotel, next to Cobh Heritage Centre, ph: (0)21 481 5566
   In Cobh are more than five B&Bs. Contact TIC.

Carrigtwohill
   B&B Dun-Vreeda House, ph: (0)21 488 3169
   B&B Casa Del Rose, Barrys Court, ph: (0)21 488 3432
   Campings: Jasmine Villa, ph: (0)21 488 3234

Map 46
Midleton
   Midleton Park Hotel And Spa, Old Cork Road, ph: (0)21 463 5100
   An Stor Hostel, Drury's Avenue, ph: (0)21 463 3106
   There are in Midleton also more than five B&Bs.
   Camping Trabolgan, ph: (0)21 466 1551

Youghal

Castlemartyr

    Hostel Castlemartyr Resort, ph: (0)21 464 4050

Map 47

Youghal

    Quality Hotel & Leisure Centre Youghal, Redbarn, ph: (0)24 93050
    Walter Raleigh Hotel, ph: (0)24 92011
    Hostel Evergreen House, The Strand, ph: (0)24 92877
    There are in Youghal more than five B&Bs. Contact TIC.
    Camping Clonvillla Clonpriest, ph: (0)24 98288

Map 48

Lismore

    Lismore house Hotel, ph: (0)58 72966. (Nice hotel)
    Ballyrafter House Hotel, ph: (0)58 54002
    B&B Beechcroft, Deerpark Road, ph: (0)58 54273
    B&B Glenribbeen Lodge, Glenribbeen, ph: (0)58 54499
    B&B Northgrove, Tourtane, ph: (0)58 54325
    B&B Pine Tree House, Ballyanchor, ph: (0)58 53282
    The Glencairn Inn, ph: (0)58 56232

Cappoquin

    The Pilgrims Rest Hotel, Mount Melleray, ph: (0)58 52917

Map 49

Clonmel

    There are in Clonmel more than 5 hotels and B&Bs. Contact TIC.

Map 50

Clonmel

    Camping Powers The Pot. Harneys Cross, Mountain Rd, ph: (0)52 23085, sharp climb over 6 km (3.7miles)

Map 51

Carrick-on-Suir

    Hotel The Carraig, ph: (0)51 641455
    B&B Fatima House, ph: (0)51 640298

Mullinavat

    Guesthouse Rising Sun, ph: (0)51 898173

Map 52

New Ross

    Brandon House Hotel And Solas Cra Spa, ph: (0)51 421703
    Macmurrough Farm Hostel, ph: (0)51 421383 (± 5km (3miles) east)
    There are more than five B&Bs in New Ross. Contact TIC.

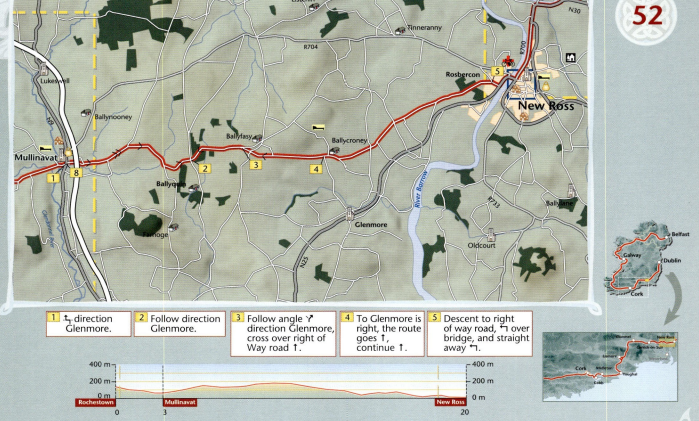

1. ↰ direction Glenmore.
2. Follow direction Glenmore.
3. Follow angle ↱ direction Glenmore, cross over right of Way road ↑.
4. To Glenmore is right, the route goes ↑, continue ↑.
5. Descent to right of way road, ↰ over bridge, and straight away ↰.

53

1. Over bridge ← (R700). After 2km road merges with N30. After 1600m over main road ← R729 direction Borris.

2. 1st turning → at Davitt Bar direction Wheelan's Bar. 1st turning ← up.

3. At right of way road ↑, after 100m keep right upwards (at V-junction, angled ⇗).

4. At right of way road ↑.

5. ← at crossing, → direction Rathmure and after 100m ← Direction Templeludigan. Afterwards continue ↑.

6. Keep to the right, not to St.Mullins. Next junction ←. Afterwards continue ↑.

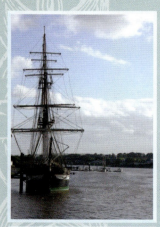

A replica of the Dunbrody, one of the ships that the Irish emigrants took to America.

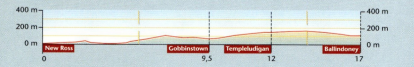

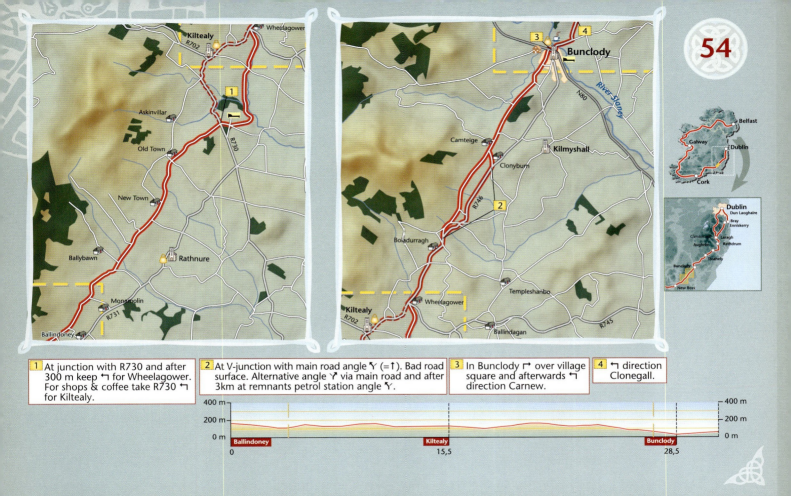

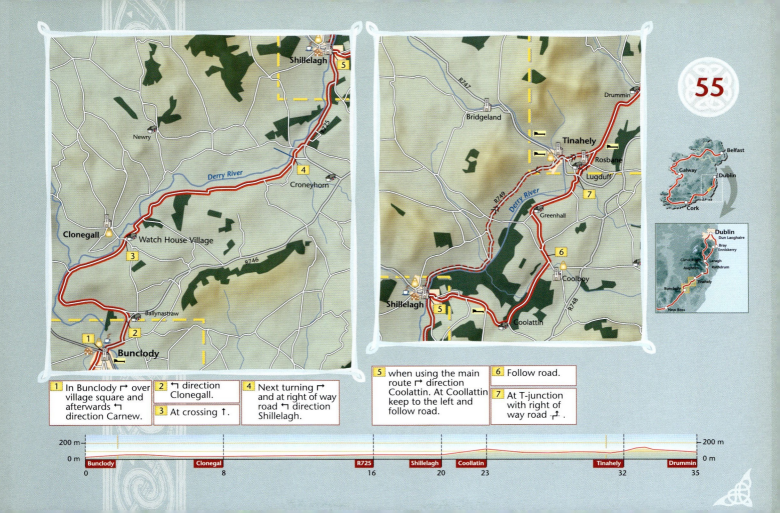

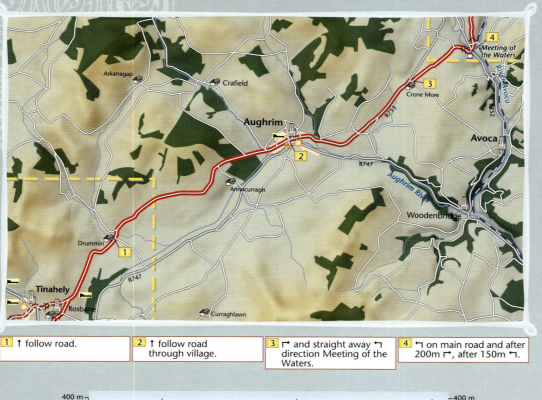

| 1 | ↑ follow road. | 2 | ↑ follow road through village. | 3 | ↱ and straight away ↰ direction Meeting of the Waters. | 4 | ↰ on main road and after 200m ↱, after 150m ↰. |

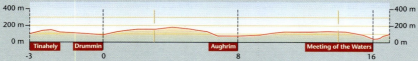

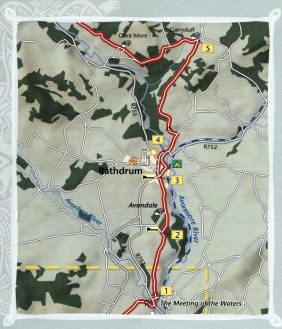

1	At Meeting of the Waters ↰ direction Rathdrum, 1st road ↱ and straight away ↰.	4	Over bridge ↰ direction Moneytown, follow asphalt road. At junction ↰.	6	Follow main road till crossing Laragh. At crossing of R115 to Sally Gap and follow to Dublin, or after 50m ↰ on to small road L1059.
2	1st road ↱ (direction Avondale).	5	At junction ↰ Laragh.	7	Keep following road.
3	In Rathdrum or through village + ↱ sharp descend. Or ↱ descend via main road.				

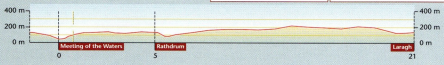

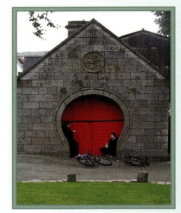

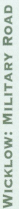

TINAHELY

AUGHRIM

GLENDALOUGH

WICKLOW: MILITARY ROAD

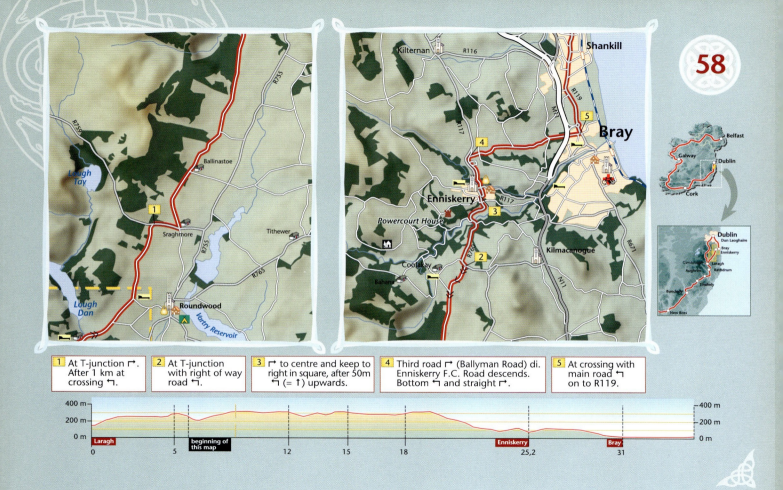

Powerscourt House & Gardens

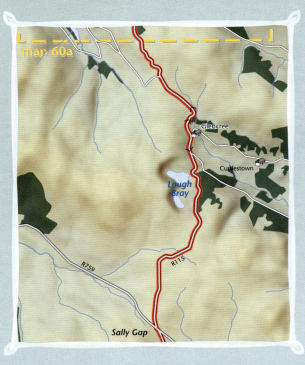

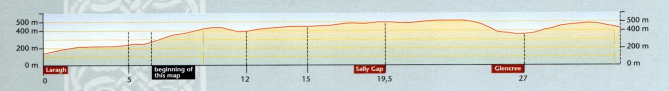

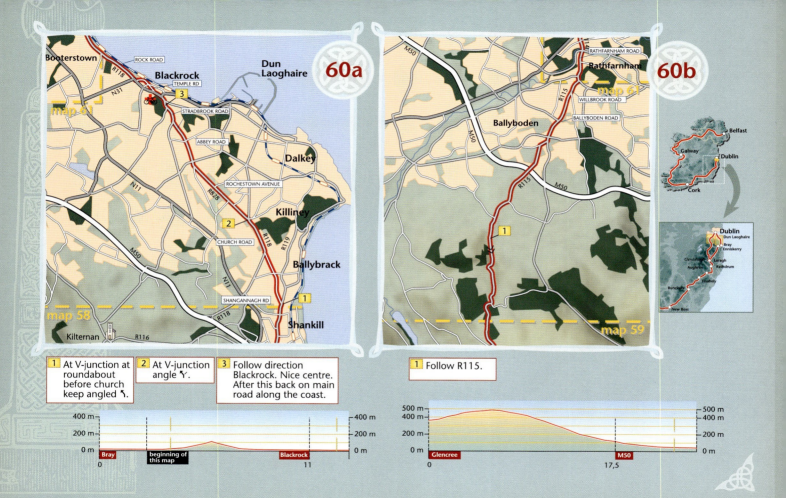

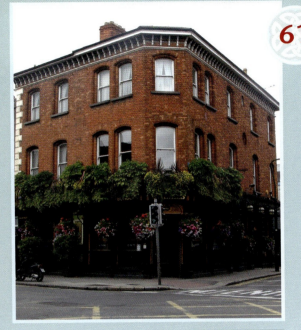

| 1 | ↱ crossing the railway. Follow road till in Dublin centre. |

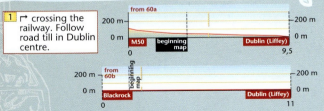

A pub in Dublin.

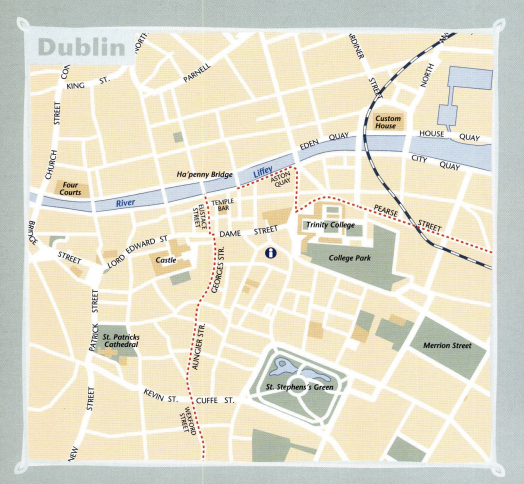

A building built by the Iveagh Trust, a social housing construction organisation.

There will always be Time for a Guinness

Cycle shops/repairs:

Cork
- Capwell Cycles, Capwell Rd, ph: (0)21 4961530
- Carroll Cycles, Dillons Cross, ph: (0)21 4508923
- Westend Cycles, West Village (Opp L&N) Ballincollig, ph: (0)21 4873804
- Rothar Cycles, 55 Barrack St, ph: (0)21 4313133
- Kilgrews Cycle Centre, 6 Kyle St, ph: (0)21 4276255
- Victoria Cross Cycles, Victoria Cross, ph: (0)21 4342240
- Douglas Cycles, 4 St Anthonys Villas Douglas West, ph: (0)21 4364340

Midleton
- An Rothar, 2 Showpark Mill Rd, ph: (0)21 4632554

Clonmel
- The Cycle Centre, 18 Irishtown, ph: (0)52 25322
- Worldwide Cycles, Hughes Mill Suir Island, ph: (0)52 21146

Carrick-on-Suir
- O K Sports, New St, ph: (0)51 640626

New Ross
- Cullens Cycles, Waterford Rd, ph: (0)51 422332

MOUNT LEINSTER, WICKLOW AND DUBLIN

There is an elongated hill ridge that runs from New Ross to Dublin and extends into the Wicklow Mountains. The ridge is interrupted only at Bunclody, near the valley of the Slaney River. The route runs in the same direction as the hill ridge, but features relatively few highs and lows once you're past the beginning. In order to get on the right track, you need to first follow a brief stretch of the busy main road from New Ross. The route then continues through quiet roads almost immediately, although you will need to make a brief, sharp ascent. I have also explored the other roads around New Ross, but their course was somewhat rougher. As soon as you arrive at the right height at Templeludigan and the weather is clear again, you will enjoy a beautiful view of the scenery. First you need to head across the bottom of the Blackstairs Mountains and then follow a stretch of a quiet regional road. On your left-hand side is the 795-metre Mount Leinster, and if you feel like it you can head to the top, as apparently it's regarded as a local Mount Ventoux. Shortly after Kiltealy, you will be able to cycle across a small road on a fork junction. However, the asphalt is so broken and full of potholes here that I doubt that the experience will be enjoyable. I have therefore provided an alternative route that will allow you to follow the regional road for another few kilometres.

Bunclody is a small, but charming, town whose centre has a rectangular square. If you turn to the left on arriving in the town and continue for several hundred metres, you will find a modern café-restaurant that serves excellent coffee.

The route then continues upstream through the Slaney valley and then past the Derry, a tributary of the River Slaney. The scenery here is picture-perfect and along the Derry you'll barely notice the ascent at all. Near Shillelagh, I decided to let the main route follow a slightly longer course across the right bank, towards Tinahely.

The direct route through Tinahely includes two slightly steeper ascents.

Tinahely is another pleasant town that offers most of the services and amenities you'll need, and after Tinahely the route continues from the Derry Valley to the Aughrim Valley, at which point you'll notice that you're approaching the highs and lows of the Wicklow Mountains. The lovely town of Aughrim has been voted 'The Cleanest Town in Ireland' numerous times: the houses and shops are in perfect condition and the parks and public grounds are equally well maintained. You certainly won't hear me complain, and in any event the meal at the local hotel-restaurant, Lawless, was excellent. You can select your food at the counter from what's on offer; meals are buffet service only – the wait staff is there only to serve drinks. There are two other restaurants, and three kilometres further down there is a restaurant that only serves regionally grown, organic food.

After Aughrim the route gradually heads up a hill, after which it slopes down more steeply, into the Avoca Valley. The Avoca River has two main branches, the Avonmore and the Avonbeg, and their confluence is referred to as 'The Meeting of the Waters', after Thomas Moore's eponymous poem:

There is not in the wide world a valley so sweet, as the vale in whose bosom the bright waters meet;
Oh, the last rays of feeling and life must depart,
Ere the bloom of that valley shall fade from my heart.

From this spot, it is easy to imagine how the he gained inspiration for his poem. I was lucky in that the water flowed in three different directions: the rain was also lashing down, and at the nearby café-restaurant they were serving hot tea and coffee. From this point the route leads slightly upward, passing Avondale, the estate that once belonged to the great 19th-century Irish political leader Charles Stewart Parnell. The Georgian estate is set in a spacious park that is open to the public. As you head slightly north you arrive in Rathdrum, a pleasant village with pubs and shops that serves as a base for people hiking in the Wicklow Mountains.

The direct road to Laragh is scenic, but also quite narrow, and since the driving speed is relatively high here it didn't seem safe enough to me to include it. As an alternative, the route now runs along a slightly longer road on the other side of the valley, offering a beautiful view of the mountains.

Laragh is located at a junction of roads to and from the Wicklow Mountains, not far from the ancient monastic town of Glendalough. The name of this town means 'Glen of Two Lakes', and this is indeed one of the most beautiful spots in the area.

Founded by St Kevin 1,200 years ago, the community evolved into a major spiritual centre that attracted people from all over Ireland and across the world. The town was sadly destroyed by English troops in the fourteenth century, after which it served for some time as a den of robbers. History aside, however, the place is magical and walking around here is an extraordinary experience.

This place is a major tourist site so there will be coachloads of tourists, along with Irish visitors. If you intend to visit, you'll need to plan it strategically.

The sights and the walking tour to the second lake located just behind are certainly worth the effort, even when it's raining.

The route splits at Laragh. The first branch leads across the old Military Road to the Sally Gap, at a height of 500 metres, straight through the Wicklow Mountains towards Dublin. The Military Road here was built by the English after the 1798 Rebellion because the area, due to its inaccessibility, had been used as a hiding place for rebels. The route will take you up along a waterfall and wooded areas covered with moss and fern, and from there to the rugged heath land above. This area looks out over the vast surrounding lateral valleys and mountaintops. The route first descends into a lateral valley near Glencree. This Wicklow village is home to the Centre for Peace and Reconciliation, which is housed in one of the old military barracks, as well as to a German war cemetery. While no Germans actually fought on Irish soil as Ireland was neutral during World War II, many soldiers who fell to their death here during air raids or who were washed ashore were buried in this cemetery.

The route leads upward one last time, and from there you'll be able to see Dublin down below, with the route descending sharply.

There are only two places in the South where the ascent into mountains takes a bit more effort; generally you can cycle at a relaxed pace and enjoy the vast scenery.

The second route leads you along the foot of the mountains to Ireland's most beautiful estate: the Powerscourt House and the surrounding Powerscourt Gardens. On the way to the estate you will first pass Lough Tay, where the route descends briefly, but sharply, only to make your way back up from the valley. The remainder of the route continues along the mountainside, with a view of the gorgeous Sugarloaf Mountain on the right. The route then descends to Enniskerry, and right before, on your left-hand side, you will see the entrance to Powerscourt House (note: there is an admission charge to access the grounds). The long driveway leads up to this elegant estate, which was acquired by the former tennis champion Michael Slazenger in 1961. A part of the estate (which was built in 1739) burnt down in 1975, but it has since been restored. The highlight of the estate, however, is not the building (which has a visitors' area and a restaurant) but rather the stunning gardens that surround it. You'll find a great variety of plants and flowers arranged in different styles, and I thought the section featuring the Japanese Garden was particularly impressive and authentic. The estate also overlooks Ireland's largest waterfall, which is a little bit farther away. Not surprisingly, Powerscourt Gardens also attracts large numbers of visitors, but you shouldn't let that hold you back, as it's definitely worth seeing.

Enniskerry, a lovely little village with a triangular square, is the last rural village before you get to Dublin (and for Dubliners on a daytrip, it's the first they see of the countryside when heading out of the city from the south side). The route then descends to the sea (after passing a small hill) and into Dublin's southern suburbs. There aren't that many accessible roads here, and since many side roads lead into a dead end the only alternative is to use the main roads. Fortunately, cycle tracks are becoming increasingly common along the main roads. The government also has a long-term plan to add more cycle routes in the future. Biking through the main shopping street in Blackrock is a nice change of pace, and via Pearse Street you'll enter the heart of Dublin at last. After Pearse Station, you will pass the walls of the renowned Trinity College. On the square that follows you can either keep left and continue on the main road (where you'll have to manoeuvre to avoid the cars) or head towards the banks of the Liffey. When you get to the Ha'penny Bridge you're really in the heart of Dublin. Time for a Guinness, I say!

Dublin is a fascinating city. From a cyclist's point of view it's a bit of a shambles, but I found it to be a good city for walking. While the city is certainly far from pretty, it makes up for its lack of beauty with its liveliness.

Accommodation

Map 54

Bunclody

The Carlton Millrace Hotel, Carrigduff, ph: (0)53 937 5100

B&B Meadowside, Ryland Street, ph: (0)53 937 6226

B&B Moss Cottage, ph: (0)53 937 7828

B&B Weston, Church Road, ph: (0)53 937 6435

Map 55

Shillelagh

Stoops Guesthouse, Stoops, Coolattin, ph: (0)53 942 9698

Map 55/56

Tinahely

B&B Rosbane Farmhouse, Rosbane, ph: (0)402 38100

B&B Kyle Farmhouse, ph: (0)59 6471341

B&B Madeline's Guest Accommodation, O'Dwyer Square, ph: (0)402 38590

B&B Sunindale House, ph: (0)402 38170

Map 56

Aughrim

Lawless Hotel, ph: (0)402 36146

B&B Butlers Byrne, Rednagh Hill, ph: (0)402 36644

B&B Kyrina, Yinnakilly, ph: (0)402 36164

B&B Macreddin Rock, ph: (0)402 36369

The Brooklodge Hotel, ph: (o)402 3644

Map 57

Rathdrum

Hostel The Old Presbytery, The Fairgreen, ph: (0)404 46930

There are in Rathdrum also more than five B&Bs. Contact TIC.

Camping Hidden Valley Holiday Park, ph: (0)404 46080

Laragh/Glendalough

Glendalough Hotel, ph: (0)404 45135

Lynham's Hotel, ph: (0)404 45345

Glendaloch International Youth Hostel, ph: (0)404 45342

B&B Glendalough Heather House, ph: (0)404 45236

B&B Bracken, ph: (0)404 45300

B&B Pinewood Lodge, ph: (0)404 45437

B&B Clondara, ph: (0)404 45417

Roundwood

B&B Wicklow Way Lodge, ph: (0)1 281 8489

B&B Loughdan House, ph: (0)1 281 7027

B&B Woodside, ph: (0)1 281 8195

Caravan and Camping Park, ph: (0)1 281 8163

Map 58

Enniskerry

   Powerscourt Arms Hotel, ph: (0)1 282 8903, pleasant village hotel

   Summerhill House Hotel, ph: (0)1 286ph: 7928

   The Ritz-Carlton Powerscourt, ph: (0)1 274 8888 (for very large budgets)

   Knockree Youth Hostel, Lackan house, ph: (0)1 286 4036

   B&B Coolakay House, ph: (0)1 286 2423

   B&B Ferndale, ph: (0)1 286 3518

   B&B Oaklawn, Glaskenny, ph: (0)1 286 0493

   B&B Twin Pines, Old Long Hill, ph: (0)1 286 0902

Bray

   There are in Bray more than five hotels and B&Bs. For more information contact TIC.

Dublin

   There is sufficient accommodation in the greater Dublin area. Contact TIC or look on our site for a comprehensive list.

CYCLE SHOPS/REPAIRS:

Enniscorthy (20 km of route)

   Kenny's For Bikes, Slaney St, ph: (0)53 923 3255

Rathmines (near Dublin)

   Think Bike, Rathmines Town Cntr, 6 Lower Rathmines Rd, ph: (0)1 496 5314

Bray

   Everest Cycles, U6 Everest Cntr, ph: (0)1 282 8660

Blackrock (near Dublin)

   Ferris Wheel Cycles, 110 Rock Rd, Blackrock, ph: (0)1 288 3819

Glendalough

Final note

While we have taken great care to ensure that the information provided is as accurate and complete as possible, this guide may contain some inaccuracies and/or omissions. Please also note that details regarding accommodation change continuously. If you are missing any information or would like to share your experiences with us, please send an e-mail to: cycling@cyclingeurope.nl.
We also welcome stories and photos from readers.

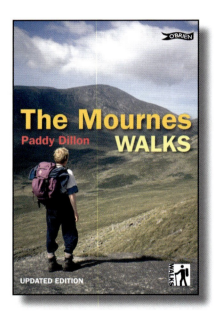

The Mournes Walks
by Paddy Dillon
Updated edition.

Where the mountains of Mourne sweep down to the sea

They sweep down to the sea, they rise in huge heathery humps, surrounded by farmlands divided into tiny, stone-walled fields. Explore the Mournes in the company of walking expert Paddy Dillon, taking in rugged coast, high mountains and forest parks. Follow the mighty Mourne Wall on its meanderings and visit the quiet corners where the history, heritage, wildlife and stillness of the area can be enjoyed.

THE WALKS
Covers all parts of the Mournes

- The High and Low Mournes as well as the Kingdom of Mourne
- The Silent Valley circuit
- The Mourne Coastal Path
- The old smuggling route of the Brandy Pad
- Warrenpoint and Rostrevor
- The complete Mourne Wall circuit
- The Mourne Trail section of the Ulster Way in four parts from Newry to Clough
- Tollymore and Castlewellan Forest Parks
- As well as lesser-known outlying trails such as the Castlewellan Loanans

West Cork Walks
by Kevin Corcoran
Updated edition with a brand new walk.

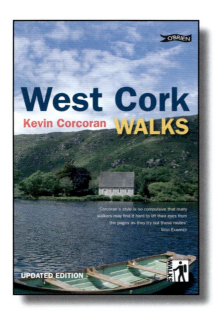

Experience the rugged wildness of Ireland's most southerly, and often considered most beautiful region, in the company of an expert naturalist. Walking in West Cork offers an incredible variety of choice - mountainous peaks, rolling heaths, forested valleys, pristine lakes and sandy beaches - the choice is yours.

WEST CORK WALKS details 10 different walks spread across West Cork, giving clear instructions with maps for each walk, the approximate length of time they should take, equipment required, notable features along the way, beautiful wildlife illustrations by the author. Casual strollers, family groups, ramblers and serious walkers are all catered for.

- LOCATION OF WALKS: The Gearagh (near Macroom), Ballyvourney, Gougane Barra, Bere Island, Castlefreke (near Rosscarbery), Lough Hyne (near Skibbereen), Mizen Head, Priest's Leap (near Glengarriff), Glengarriff and Allihies

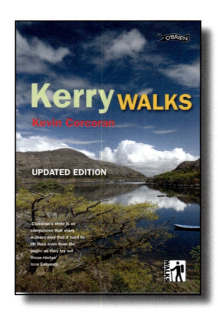

Kerry Walks
by Kevin Corcoran
Updated edition.

The perfect walking guide to the wilderness and beauty of Kerry

Discover the landscape and wildlife of Ireland's most beautiful county with walking enthusiast and expert naturalist Kevin Corcoran. These twenty walks explore heathland and bog, Ireland's highest mountains, coastal peninsulas, beaches, islands, forests, rivers, lakes.

THE WALKS

- Lough Acoose, Bray Head, Lough Currane, Derrynane, Rossbeigh, Anascaul, Ballydavid, Great Blasket Island, Mount Eagle, The Magharees, Kenmare Uplands, Barraboy Ridge

SPECIAL KILLARNEY SECTION

- Muckross, The Paps, Mangerton, Torc Mountain, Knockreer, Old Kenmare Road, Crohane, Tomies Wood
- IDEAL for casual strollers, family groups, ramblers and serious walkers
- Clear, detailed instructions – beautiful wildlife illustrations – location maps – information on flora and fauna

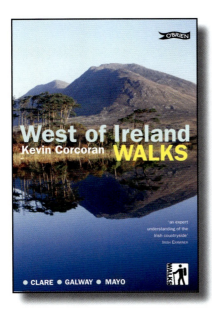

West of Ireland Walks
by Kevin Corcoran

Explore the counties of Clare, Galway and Mayo in the company of a wildlife expert.

The West of Ireland offers a huge choice of landscape to the walker - mountain peaks, woodland, bogs and lakes, sandy beaches and the strange limestone plateaux of the Burren.

- *Contains 14 walks spread across the West.*
- *Includes clear, detailed instructions and location maps, with each walk outlined.*
- *Features wildlife illustrations and information on flora and fauna.*
- *Caters for casual strollers, family groups, and ramblers, as well as serious walkers.*